A MARY FORD PUBLICATION

MAKING
TEDDY BEARS

ACKNOWLEDGEMENTS

Mary Ford acknowledges with grateful thanks the creative contribution of Anne Sexton, who designed and made the Teddy Bears in this book. She also wishes to thank her husband, Michael Ford, who photographed and edited the book.

AUTHORS

Mary Ford's expertise and artistry are well known from her best-selling series of Cake Decorating Books, which has now been extended into other popular crafts. Mary remembers with great affection the cuddly companion of her childhood, a much loved Teddy with a chewed ear! She has now adopted Edward, a Teddy Bear Doorstop made by Anne Sexton, to hold open her lounge door. Mary has always had an interest in all crafts and was delighted to collaborate once again with Anne in creating this exciting range of Teddy Bears.

Professional toy-maker Anne Sexton has turned an absorbing hobby into a successful career. Unable to purchase the kind of toys she wanted for her children, she created them herself and was soon inundated with orders. She now exhibits extensively at Craft Fairs all over the South of England and her Teddies travel all over the world.

OTHER MARY FORD TITLES

ISBN 0 946429 32 4

COPYRIGHT 1990 Mary Ford Publications Limited
Published by Mary Ford Publications Limited, 294b Lymington Road, Highcliffe on Sea, Christchurch, Dorset BH23 5ET, England.

Printed and bound in Hong Kong

PAGE 54

PAGE 77

Contents

PAGE 68

PAGE 86

PAGE 62

PAGE 12

PAGE 44

PAGE 28

PAGE 13

PAGE 37

☆ STAR RATINGS ☆

All Teddy Bears are graded for ease of making, one star being suitable for beginners through to four and five stars for the experienced soft toy-maker

PAGE 21

Introduction

TEDDY Bears are a perennial favourite with children. In this stimulating book eleven brand new Teddy Bear designs are featured, ranging from traditional, modern and jointed Teddies to innovative doorstop, shoulder bag and hot water bottle cover Bears. All are in my well-known pictorial step-by-step format and are accompanied by full-size templates. A preliminary section introduces the inexperienced toy-maker to all the techniques required for trouble-free sewing and each Teddy is carefully graded for ease of making.

The traditional Teddy Bear has a thin body with a pronounced hump, very long arms and legs, and a triangular head with a pointed nose. Original bears were firmly stuffed with straw or sawdust and many had glass button eyes (which, unfortunately, soon became detached and could easily be eaten by children). Anne has designed a traditional Teddy Bear in modern, authentic, mohair material, using stuffing, eyes and joints to reach the safety standards required for children's toys today.

The modern design of Teddy Bear has a very much more rounded face with a flat nose, a fat body and shorter arms and legs. They look remarkably cheerful – in contrast to some of the traditional bears – and are extremely cuddly and appealing for children. They have a lazy air about them, as if simply waiting for their owner.

The History of the Teddy Bear

TEDDY Bears made their appearance prior to The First World War and they quickly became treasured childhood companions. Although no-one has ever been able to quite explain their appeal, they have never lost their place in the hearts of children – or adults.

According to American sources, the first Teddy Bear was based on a cartoon by Clifford Berryman that appeared in the *Washington Post* in 1903. The cartoon featured President 'Teddy' Roosevelt on a bear hunt in the Rocky Mountains, with a small bear cub at his feet. An enterprising toy manufacturer, Morris Michtom of the Ideal Toy Corporation quickly wrote to the President asking permission to call a small bear cub 'Teddy's bear'. The President willingly gave permission although he did not think that his name would be worth much to the toy bear cub business.

Mrs Michtom, herself a talented needlewoman, made the first samples, including one which was sent to the President. The new toy quickly caught on and was manufactured, in a slightly different style, by the Steiff Company of Germany. Their bear had much longer, thinner limbs and early examples are greatly prized by arctophiles (Teddy Bear collectors) who pay a high price for their acquisitions.

The Steiff Bear was based on a sketch made at Stuttgart Zoo by Franz Steiff, an art student. He persuaded his Aunt, Margarete Steiff to make the bears. Paralysed by polio, she was confined to a wheelchair and had made her living as a seamstress. Her hobby was making small toy felt elephants for the local children and these became so popular that the family set up a toy factory. The success of the Steiff bears can be gauged by the fact that in 1903 they made 12,000 bears but by 1907 this had risen to 974,000.

The Steiff family have their own version of how the bears came to be called Teddy. According to them, early Steiff bears were used to decorate the tables at the wedding reception of President Roosevelt's daughter. When asked what sort of bears they were, the enchanted President is reputed to have said 'Teddies, of course'. Prior to that they had been known simply as 'Bruin'.

Tools and Materials

TOOLS

Aᴌᴌ the Teddy Bears in this book were sewn with an ordinary domestic sewing machine. Most of the tools required will be found in a dressmaker's kit but improvisations can sometimes be made – a knitting needle can be used as a stuffing tool, for instance, and cereal boxes will provide thin card if required.

Good, sharp scissors of the correct size are vital, however. A pair of dressmaker's scissors are required for cutting fabric and small embroidery scissors are useful. An old pair of scissors should always be used to cut card as otherwise good scissors will quickly become blunt.

Tracing paper is required for transferring the templates to durable card, and a felt-tip pen can be used for tracing but should not be used on fabric. A 2B lead pencil should be used for marking light coloured fabric and tailor's chalk for dark.

In the interests of safety, pins and needles should always be counted before and after use. Extra long, glass-headed pins are the most suitable and a medium sized needle is required for hand sewing. A darning or embroidery needle will facilitate the sewing on of heads, limbs or facial features. For machine use, a No. 16 or 18 needle is the most durable.

Although most shapes can be stuffed by hand, a pencil, screwdriver or the blunt end of a knitting needle is helpful for small pieces.

Fur fabric pile requires brushing with a teazle brush after handling to bring up the pile or to free pile trapped in the seam after sewing.

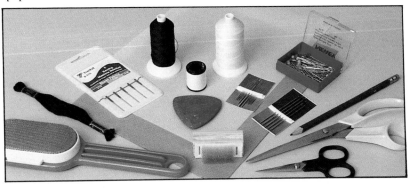

MATERIALS

Mᴀᴛᴇʀɪᴀʟs should always be selected for quality, durability and appeal. The character of the finished Teddy will be enhanced by the use of an appropriate colour and texture. When purchasing materials, it is important to ensure that they comply with the regulations for the safety of children's toys.

The fur fabric chosen for Teddy Bears should have a supple, knitted back as this stretches slightly and does not fray. A dense pile through which the backing does not show indicates a good quality fur. However, mohair, which is used for the traditional Teddy has a very firm backing and does not stretch. This makes it more difficult to sew and beginners may find that plush fur fabric is more suitable, particularly as mohair is much more expensive than the other furs. Mohair does, however, produce an excellent high quality finish and experienced needlewomen will find that it is well worth the extra money.

○ **Polished fur** has a short shiny pile.

○ **Plush fur** has a thicker, shorter pile.

○ **Super fur** has long, soft, fluffy pile which does not lie flat.

○ **Mohair** is made from the hair of a Tibetan goat and has a short dense pile. It is the traditional Teddy Bear material.

○ **Felt** is available in many colours and is used for paws, facial features or clothes. Polyester felt, whilst not a strong material, is useful as it can be washed.

○ **Lining.** Soft cotton material should be used for lining.

○ **Filling.** Hi Loft polyester filling is ideal as it is washable, springy and non-allergic.

○ **Thread.** A toning strong synthetic thread should be used for sewing seams as this will not break when the Teddy is turned. Button, or extra-strong, thread should be used for hand sewing. Stranded embroidery thread is used for facial features.

NOTE: Throughout this book, a contrasting thread has been used for photographic purposes. Matching thread should be used when sewing the Teddy Bears.

Pattern Making

A LL the templates in this book are full size and ready for transferring onto card, as shown in steps 1-3. *EDWARD BEAR* is used here but the principle is exactly the same for all patterns. It is important to transfer all markings, instructions, etc., from the template onto the pattern. The completed pattern should be stored in a clearly labelled envelope or paper bag.

NOTE: Some of the templates in this book are drawn inside another one, or overlapping, due to restrictions on space. Each one should be traced onto a separate sheet. Do not cut a smaller template out from inside a larger one.

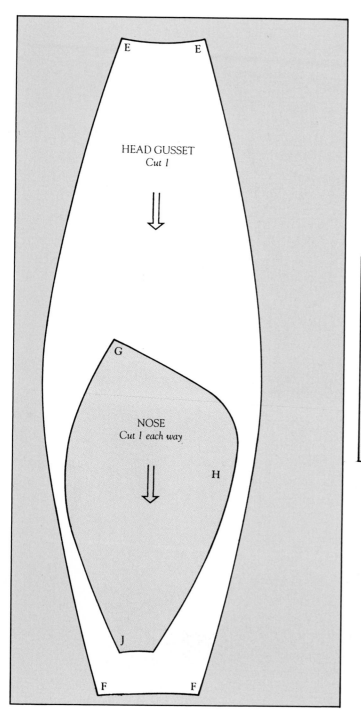

PATTERN LAYOUT

A suitable piece of fabric should be selected and checked for direction of pile. When a hand is run across the fabric, in one direction the pile will be raised up from the surface of the fabric, in the other it will be smooth. Turn the fabric over, pile side to the table, and mark with an arrow the direction in which the pile lies smoothly. Fur fabric should always be cut through one thickness only but felt and lining can be cut on a double thickness. Place the fabric on the table so that the arrow points towards you. The Teddy Bear will then appear to 'stand up' when the pattern is laid out on the fabric. The selvedge edge should not be used.

Ensure that all the patterns lie in the same direction by matching the arrows on the pattern to the arrow indicating direction of the pile on the fabric. The larger pieces should be positioned first and then the smaller pieces fitted in (in accordance with the direction of the pile). Check that all pattern pieces are positioned correctly and that nothing has been omitted. Draw round the patterns with a soft pencil or chalk depending on the colour of the fabric (this is the cutting line).

Cut very carefully round each pattern with sharp scissors by sliding the point of the blade under the pile of fur fabric and cutting through the backing. Separate the pieces gently to avoid pulling the pile. Small openings or holes should be cut with embroidery scissors to ensure accuracy.

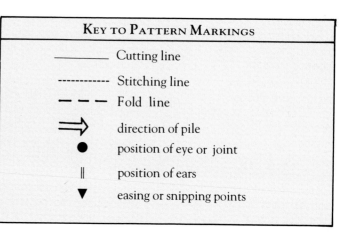

KEY TO PATTERN MARKINGS

——————— Cutting line

-------------- Stitching line

— — — Fold line

⟹ direction of pile

● position of eye or joint

‖ position of ears

▼ easing or snipping points

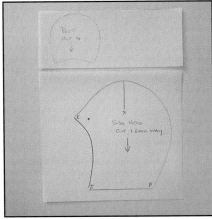

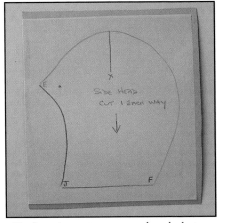

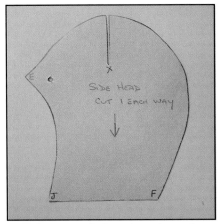

1 Trace the chosen template onto tracing paper, using a pencil or felt-tip pen. Take care that all the markings are transferred.

2 Leaving a space around each shape, roughly cut out the shapes from the tracing paper and glue the pieces onto card.

3 Cut out each shape from the card along the pencil lines. Check once again that all the markings have been transferred.

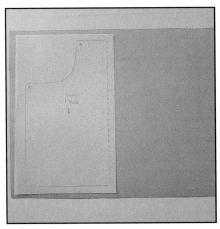

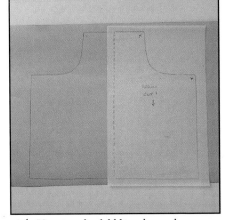

TO TRACE FOLD-LINE PIECES:
4 Lay traced template face down onto card, with markings facing the card and the fold line down the centre. Draw around the shape, omitting fold line.

5 Keeping the fold line down the centre of the card, carefully turn over the tracing paper pattern and glue into position.

6 Cut the pattern from the card as one piece.

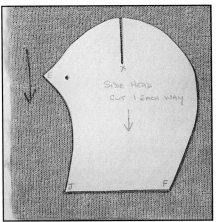

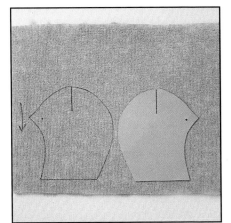

TO CUT 1 EACH WAY:
7 Place pattern onto a single thickness of fabric with the arrow lying along the grain or nap of the fabric. Draw around the pattern, as shown.

8 Reverse the shape by turning the pattern over, and draw round the pattern again. Cut out the 2 shapes along the cutting lines.

TO CUT 2 OR MORE:
9 Lay pattern onto single thickness fabric and draw around it. With same side facing, lay pattern on fabric again and draw round. Cut out both pieces.

Sewing Techniques

THE seam allowance on pattern pieces is 6mm (¼") and seams can be sewn by hand or by machine. An ordinary domestic sewing machine was used for all the Teddy Bears in this book, which were finished by hand. All the step-by-step instructions contain a detailed sewing guide for each bear.

STITCHES

○ **Running stitch** is used for gathering. Double thread should be used for extra strength and the ends should be finished with a backstitch to secure firmly.

○ **Backstitch** is used for hand-sewing seams as it produces a strong seam that will not break. The end should be knotted firmly and thread can be used double for extra strength.

○ **Ladder stitch** is used for closing openings after stuffing and for securing the head in place. When correctly sewn, this stitch is extremely strong and virtually invisible. A strong synthetic thread should be used (see below).

○ **Zigzag** or **oversewing stitch** should be used to prevent fabric fraying.

SEAMS

Beginners should pin seams with extra long glass-headed pins and then tack before sewing. In the step-by-step photographs, the seams were pinned and then sewn. Although the seams in the photographs have not been finished off, when sewing it is important to reverse the stitching for approximately 6mm (¼") at the start and end of each seam to ensure that they do not open. Matching thread should be used for stitching seams.

The steps for sewing a seam are illustrated below (steps 1-3). Curved or angled seams may need to be snipped to the stitching line in order to ease the seam. Care should be taken not to cut the stitching line.

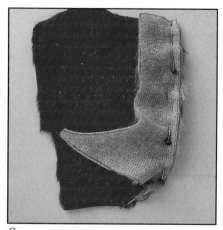

SEAMS

1 Carefully pin pieces to be sewn, right sides facing, 6mm (¼") in from the fabric edge.

2 Begin sewing 6mm (¼") below top edge. Reverse stitch to top, then sew the seam removing pins as necessary. Reverse stitch 6mm (¼") at end.

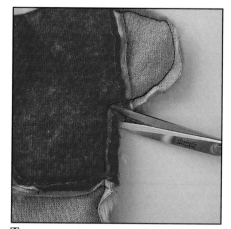

TO EASE A SEAM

3 Carefully snip to stitching line, taking care not to cut the thread.

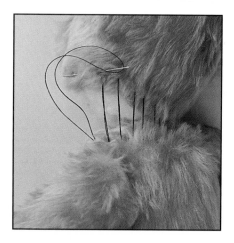

LADDER STITCH

Start sewing at the beginning and to one side of the opening. Bring the needle through from the underside of the fabric, then take the needle over the gap and make a stitch about 6mm (¼") long on the other side, starting level with the original stitch and working parallel to the opening. Then take the needle back across the opening and repeat, pulling the stitches up firmly. Finish with small backstitches.

JOINTS

Jointed Teddy Bears with moveable arms and legs, and heads that swivel from side to side, greatly add to the appeal and play potential of the toy for children. The old style of joints were very complicated as they required a cotter pin and discs. However, the new style joint available today is simple to fix and is readily available in handicraft shops.

A joint with a diameter appropriate to the size of the Teddy Bear should be selected. When attaching a limb, the limb should be sewn and stuffed half way first, leaving the top of the seam open. Insert peg from inside the limb through the joint hole. The stuffing should then be completed and the seam closed with ladder stitch. Attach the limb to the body as shown in steps 1-6 below.

When attaching the head, run a gathering stitch around the neck opening. Insert joint into the neck opening, leaving the peg outside, and pull up the gathering thread tightly. Fix the head to the body by pushing the peg through the small opening in the top of the body, securing with plastic and metal safety washers (see page 60, steps 35-37).

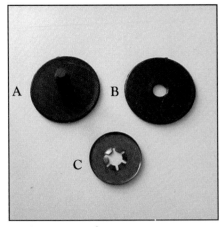

1 A — joint with peg. B — Plastic washer. C — Metal safety washer. All three sections are required for each limb or head to be attached.

2 Sew a running stitch around the hole position on the body and on the limb. Carefully snip the hole with sharp, pointed scissors.

3 Insert the joint A into the limb, working from the wrong side of the fabric, so that the peg protrudes through to the right side as shown.

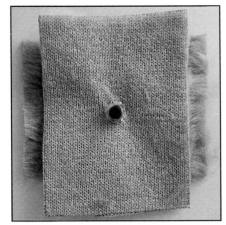

4 Insert the peg, working from the right side of the fabric, into the hole in the body as shown.

5 Place the plastic washer B over the peg and push down firmly until locked.

6 Place the metal safety washer C onto the peg and push down as far as possible. Ensure that it is level.

TURNING AND STUFFING

All seams should be carefully inspected prior to turning to ensure that there are no holes. If necessary, fix the eyes in place before turning and stuffing.

To turn the Teddy, carefully turn the limbs, using the fingers or a blunt stuffing tool, and then, if necessary, ease through the

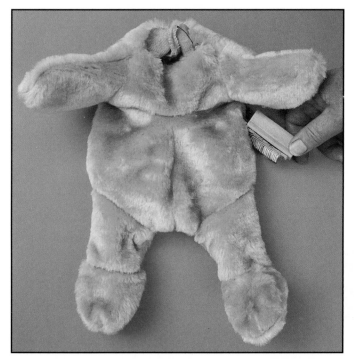

opening in the body. Turn the head as instructed and insert the nose if required.

If stuffing a jointed Teddy Bear, stuff the limbs and then attach to the body (see page 9). When stuffing bears without jointed limbs, push small amounts of filling to the ends of the

limbs with the fingers or a blunt stuffing tool. Gradually fill the limbs and then the body. Particular attention should be paid to where the limbs join the body as too much stuffing will cause the limbs to splay out and insufficient filling will cause the limbs to wobble. The head should be stuffed and attached to the body with ladder stitch, as specified in the step-by-step instructions for each bear. Use sufficient stuffing for a firm, not hard, finish — bearing in mind that the stuffing will soften when the bear is handled. After stuffing, close the opening with ladder stitch (see page 8).

FACIAL FEATURES

The finished expression of the Teddy Bear will depend on how the facial features are positioned. Bears can be made to look happy or sorrowful, alert or sleepy by careful selection and placing of the eyes and mouth, and the appeal of a Teddy can be

greatly enhanced by attractive features. 'Glass' eyes give a lively twinkle to Teddy Bears but the black 'shoe-button' eyes add a very traditional air to a bear.

The old fashioned 'sew-on' type of glass or button eyes should, however, never be used for children's toys. A wide variety of safety eyes and noses are available from handicraft shops and an appropriate size should be selected.

Fur fabric stretches and the area around the eye or nose should be reinforced by oversewing or by sticking a small piece of fabric over the area with latex adhesive before fitting safety eyes or noses. This will prevent children from pulling out the eyes or nose.

Facial features can also be embroidered with stranded embroidery cotton (see opposite) or made from small pieces of felt. An upturned mouth will make the Teddy appear to smile, whilst a downturned mouth gives a more serious nature to the bear.

FITTING SAFETY EYES AND NOSES:
1 Teddy eyes
2 Assorted noses
3 Badge
4 Washers

1 Make a very small hole, with sharp scissors, at the eye or nose position marked, and stitch round the hole to stop the hole from spreading.

2 Push the shank through from the right side of the material. Turn to right side of material and check position on the face. The position cannot be changed after step *3*.

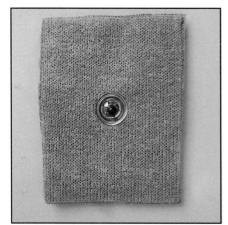

3 Turn to wrong side and place washer over shank. Lock washer against back of eye by pressing down hard, keeping the washer level, to engage the teeth of the washer against the shank.

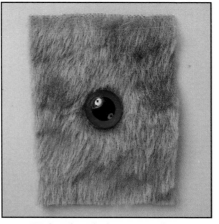

4 With right side facing, gently ease out any fur which has become trapped.

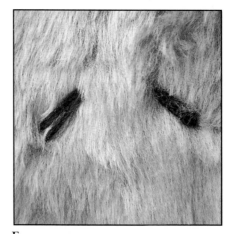

EMBROIDERING FACIAL FEATURES.
Eyes
Make two long parallel stitches at each eye point.

Mouth
Make a long stitch at the outer corner of the mouth. From the middle of this stitch, make a long stitch to centre mouth. Repeat for second side to complete the smile.

Nose and Mouth
Make a series of long parallel stitches close together to form the nose, slightly decreasing size at ends. Repeat. Make two long, angled stitches as shown for the mouth.

Teddy Mouth
Bring needle out at top of nose, embroider a straight line down. Insert needle and come out one-third of the way to the left as shown. Take needle back to bottom of the long stitch and repeat for right side.

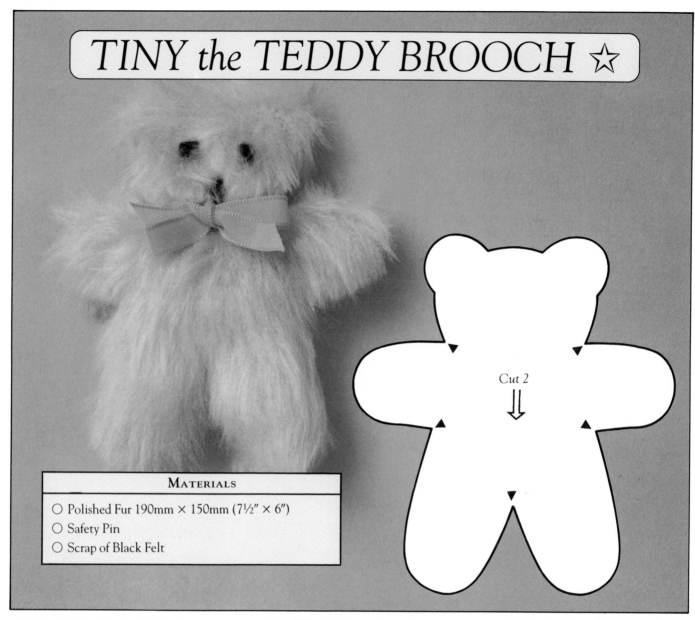

TINY the TEDDY BROOCH ☆

Cut 2

MATERIALS

○ Polished Fur 190mm × 150mm (7½″ × 6″)
○ Safety Pin
○ Scrap of Black Felt

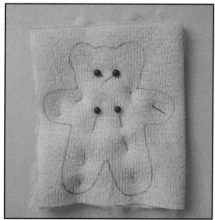

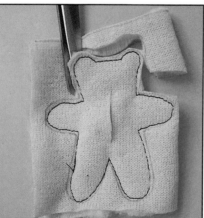

1 Fold the fabric, right sides facing and pin. Using the template as a guide, draw the teddy bear shape onto the wrong side of the fabric, as shown.

2 Stitch just inside the drawn line and cut out. Make an opening in one layer of fabric only, as shown. Snip seams at ease points and turn right sides out.

3 Lightly stuff with filling and stitch up opening. Sew on small pieces of felt for the face. Stitch a safety pin on the back and attach a bow under the chin.

CUDDLES *the* TEDDY BEAR ☆☆☆

MATERIALS
○ Super White Fur 430mm × 350mm (17″ × 14″)
○ 1 Cuddle-me Badge
○ 1 Large Heart Nose
○ 2 Teddy Eyes

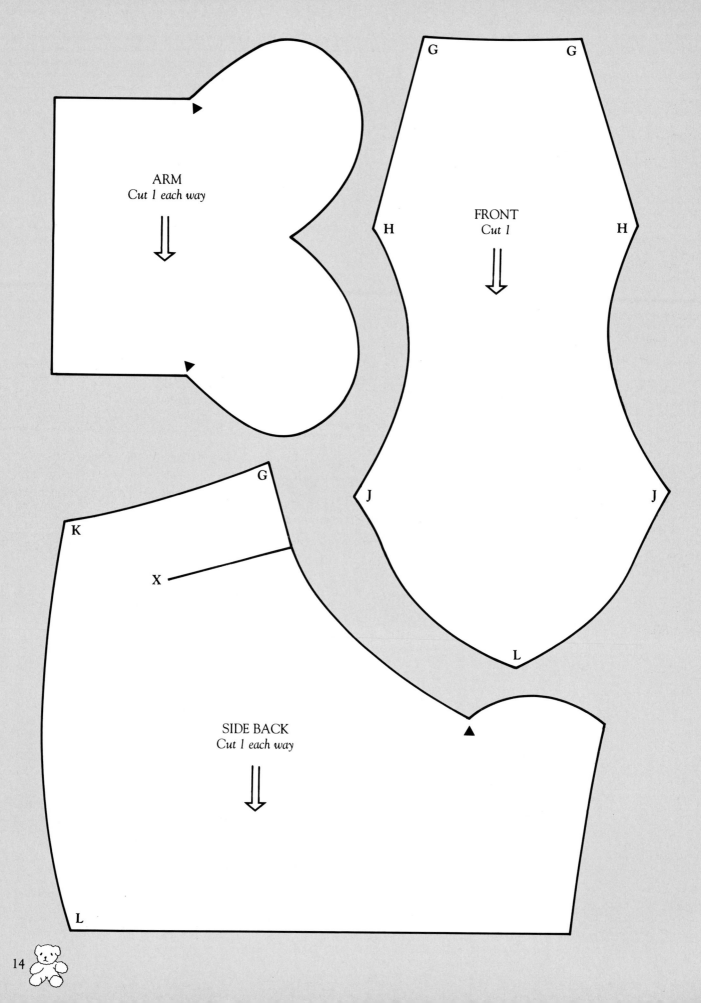

ARM
Cut 1 each way

FRONT
Cut 1

G   G

H   H

J   J

L

SIDE BACK
Cut 1 each way

G

K

X

L

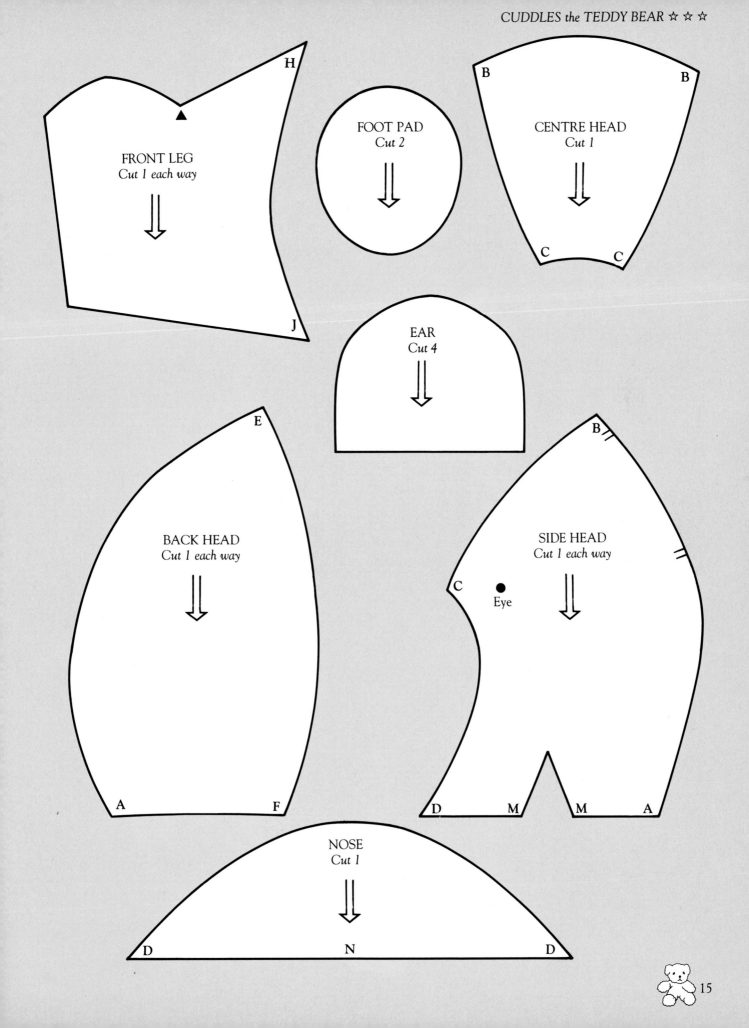

FRONT LEG
Cut 1 each way

FOOT PAD
Cut 2

CENTRE HEAD
Cut 1

EAR
Cut 4

BACK HEAD
Cut 1 each way

SIDE HEAD
Cut 1 each way

Eye

NOSE
Cut 1

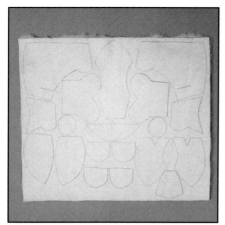

1 Make a pattern (see pages 6-7) and draw around it on the wrong side of the fabric, as shown.

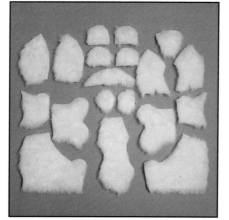

2 Cut out all the pieces and check with the picture that all the sections are there.

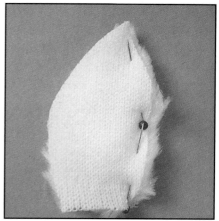

3 With right sides facing, pin back head pieces together from **F** to **E**.

4 Stitch back head together from **E** to **F**.

5 With right sides facing, pin and stitch the ears together, leaving the straight edges open.

6 Turn the ears right side out and brush the seams.

7 Fold the side head in half. Pin and stitch the dart, matching **M** to **M**, as shown.

8 With right sides facing, pin centre head to side head from **C** to **B**.

9 Stitch centre head to side head along the seam line and brush the seam.

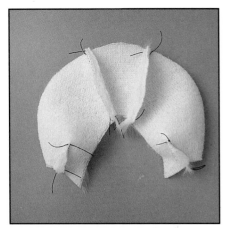

10 Repeat steps *7-9* for the second side head.

11 Turn right side up and, with right sides facing, pin nose to side head starting at **D**.

12 Upturn, then continue pinning along the edge to match second **D**.

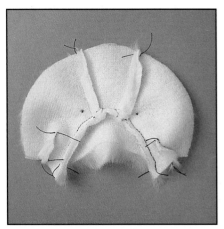

13 Carefully stitch the nose to the head along the seam line, as shown.

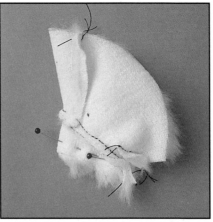

14 With right sides facing, fold the face in half and pin from **N** to **D**.

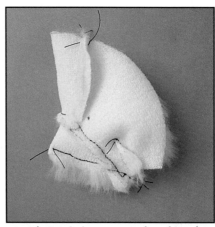

15 Stitch the nose together along the seam line and brush the seam.

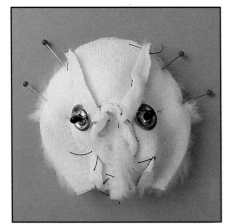

16 Unfold the head and insert the eyes (see page 11). With right sides facing, pin the ears to the face in the positions marked on the template.

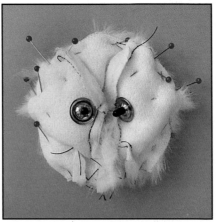

17 With right sides facing, pin back head to head, matching at **A**, and leaving the bottom edge open.

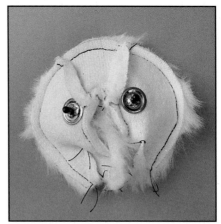

18 Carefully stitch around the head, as shown. Check that the ears are secured in the stitching line.

17

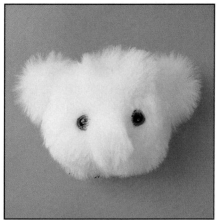

19 Turn the head right side out and brush all the seams.

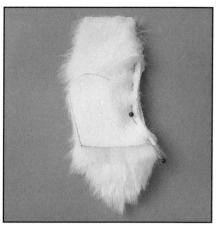

20 With right sides facing, pin front leg to front from **J** to **H**.

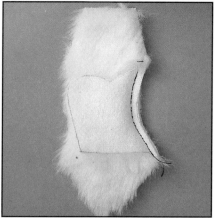

21 Stitch the front leg to front along the seam line, tapering off at the ends, as shown.

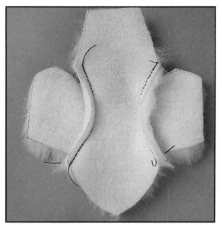

22 Repeat steps *20-21* for the second front leg.

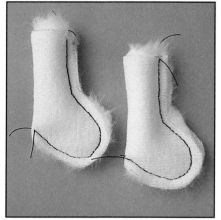

23 With right sides facing, fold the arm pieces in half, pin and stitch.

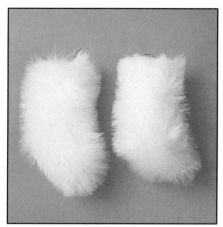

24 Turn the arms right side out and brush the seams.

25 Lightly stuff each arm with suffi-cient filling for a soft finish.

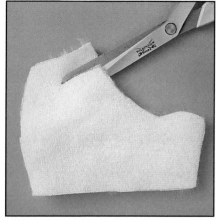

26 Cut a side back to **X** as marked on the template.

27 With right sides facing, pin an arm to the cut edge. Fold over and pin the top, as shown.

28 *Stitch arm in position, tapering off at end of stitching, as shown.*

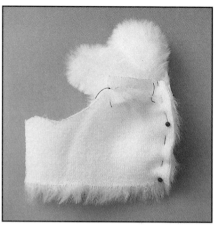

29 *Repeat steps 26-28 for second side back and arm. With right sides facing, pin together from L to K.*

30 *Stitch the side back pieces together, then unfold, as shown.*

31 *With right sides facing, carefully pin front to back, matching all letters on the templates.*

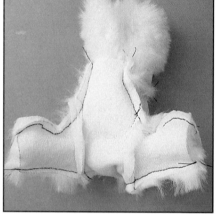

32 *Stitch the front to side back along the seam line, leaving front legs and neck open.*

33 *With right sides facing, pin a foot pad to a leg opening. Repeat for second foot pad.*

34 *Stitch each foot pad in position, making the circle as even as possible.*

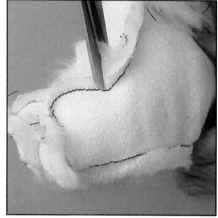

35 *Carefully snip the seams at all ease points.*

36 *Turn right side out, brush all seams and insert a heart motif in position shown.*

37 Stuff the legs and body with sufficient filling to keep the bear soft and cuddly.

38 Insert the nose and embroider the mouth (see page 11). Lightly stuff the head with filling.

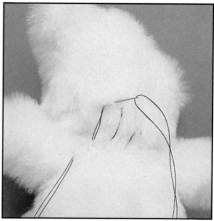

39 Attach the head to the body with ladder stitch (see page 8). Pull up firmly and secure. Add a bow of ribbon round the bear's neck for the finishing touch.

TOMBOY TED ☆☆

MATERIALS
○ Antelope Polished Fur 610mm × 305mm (24″ × 12″)
○ Cream Polished Fur 150mm × 100mm (6″ × 4″)
○ Yellow Felt 305mm × 255mm (12″ × 10″)
○ 2 Buttons
○ 2 Medium Teddy Eyes
○ 1 Small Heart Nose

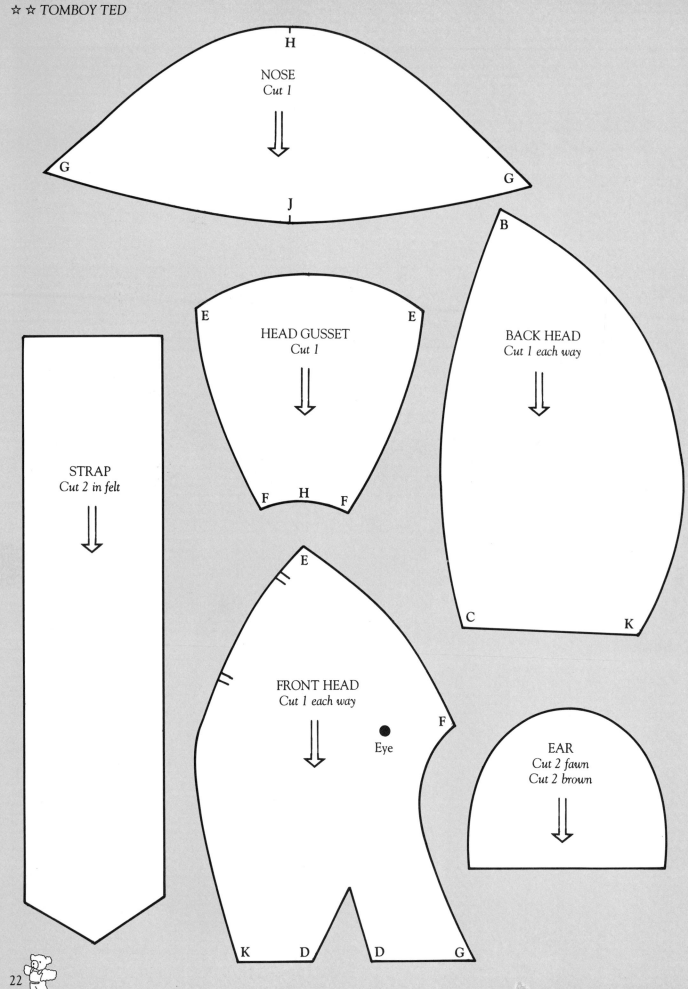

NOSE
Cut 1

H

G   G

J

HEAD GUSSET
Cut 1

E   E

F   H   F

BACK HEAD
Cut 1 each way

B

C   K

STRAP
Cut 2 in felt

FRONT HEAD
Cut 1 each way

E

F

● Eye

EAR
Cut 2 fawn
Cut 2 brown

K   D   D   G

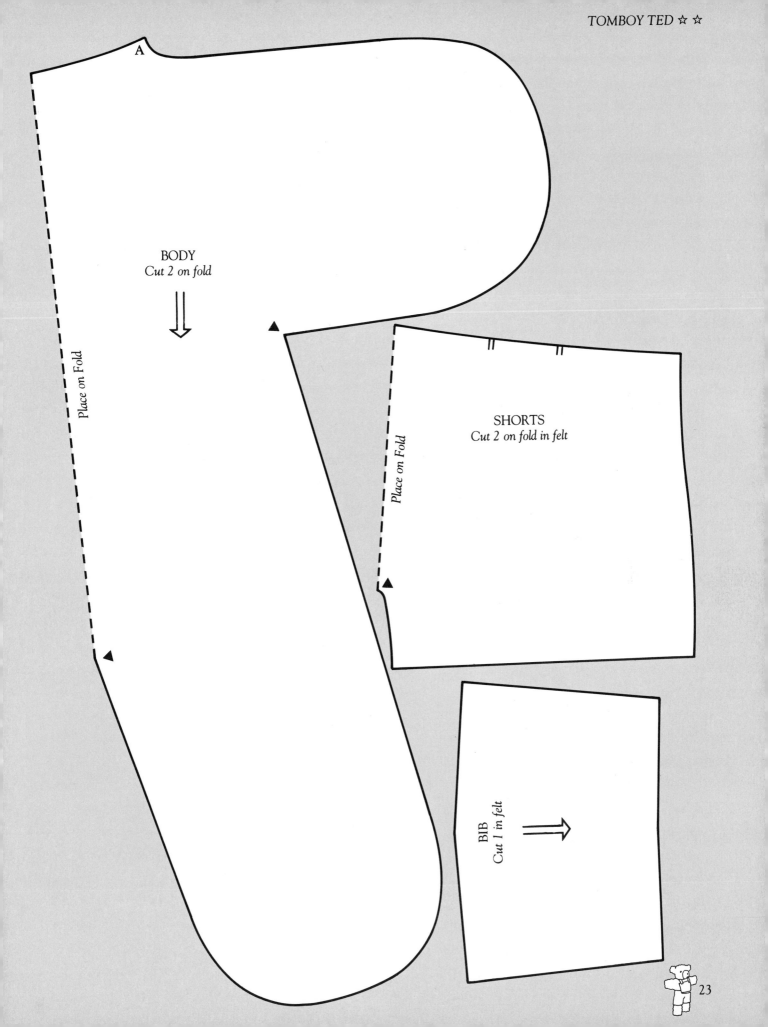

A

BODY
Cut 2 on fold

⇓

Place on Fold

SHORTS
Cut 2 on fold in felt

Place on Fold

BIB
Cut 1 in felt

⇒

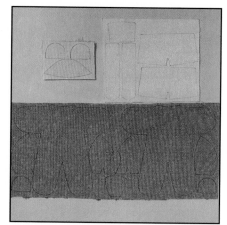

1 Make a pattern (see pages 6-7) and draw around it on the wrong side of the appropriately coloured fabric, as shown.

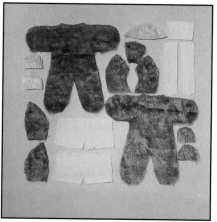

2 Cut out all the pieces and check with the picture that all the sections are there.

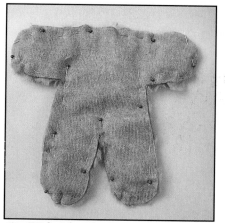

3 With right sides facing, pin the body together from **A** to **A**, leaving the neck open.

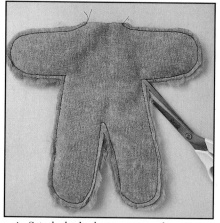

4 Stitch the body pieces together. Snip the seams at ease points.

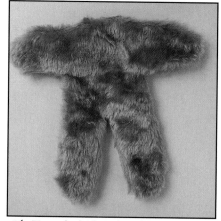

5 Turn the body right side out and brush the seams.

6 With right sides facing, pin the back head pieces together from **B** to **C**.

7 Stitch the back head pieces together along the seam line and brush the seam.

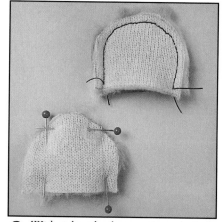

8 With right sides facing, pin and stitch the ear pieces together, leaving the straight edges open.

9 Turn the ears right sides out and brush the seams.

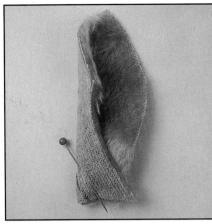

10 Pin the dart in the front head, matching **D** to **D**.

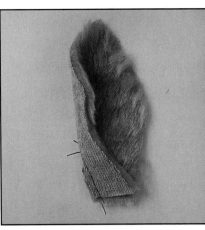

11 Stitch the dart, tapering off as shown. Brush the seams.

12 With right sides facing, pin head gusset to front head from **E** to **F**.

13 Stitch head gusset to front head. Repeat steps *12-13* for second front head.

14 With right sides facing, pin nose to front head from **G** to **H** and **H** to **G**.

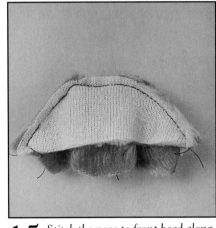

15 Stitch the nose to front head along the seam line and brush the seam.

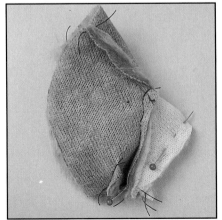

16 Fold the nose in half and pin from **J** to **G**.

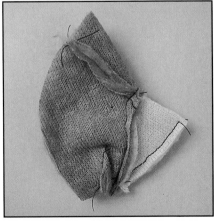

17 Stitch from **J** to **G**. Turn right side out and brush the seam.

18 Insert the eyes and nose and embroider a mouth (see page 11).

19 With right sides facing, pin the ears to the face in the positions marked on the template.

20 With right sides facing, pin back head to front head, matching **K** to **K**.

21 Stitch back head to front head. Turn right side out and brush the seam.

22 Stuff the body and head with filling until firm, but not too hard.

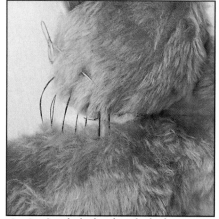

23 Stitch the head to the body using ladder stitch (see page 8) and secure. Brush the seams.

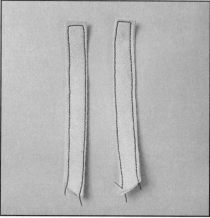

24 Fold the felt straps in half and stitch, as shown.

25 Stitch around three sides of the bib, as shown.

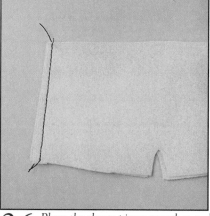

26 Place the shorts pieces together and stitch down one side seam.

27 Pin the straps to the back shorts, as marked on the template. Pin the bib to the front shorts, as shown.

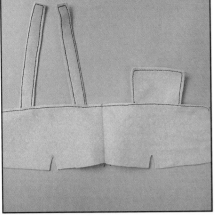  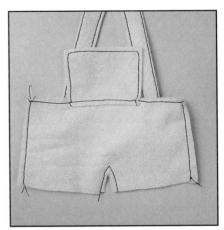

28 Stitch along the top of the shorts to secure the straps and bib.

29 Re-fold the shorts and pin down the other side seam. Pin the crotch seam.

30 Stitch side seam and crotch. Snip at ease point and turn right side out. Dress the Tomboy bear and secure the straps to the bib with buttons.

TINY TED ☆☆☆☆

MATERIALS
○ Gold Plush Fur 560mm × 305mm (22″ × 12″)
○ 2 Medium Teddy Eyes
○ 1 Small Heart Nose
○ 4 Small Joints
○ Ribbon 455mm (18″)

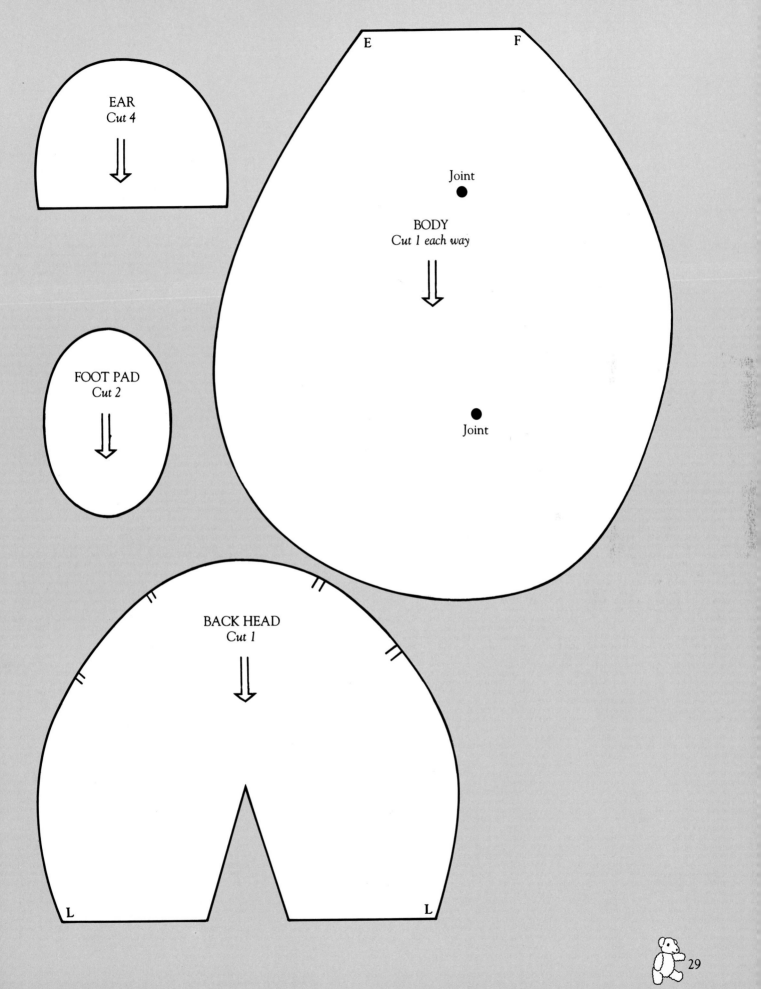

EAR
Cut 4

E   F

Joint ●

BODY
Cut 1 each way

FOOT PAD
Cut 2

● Joint

BACK HEAD
Cut 1

L   L

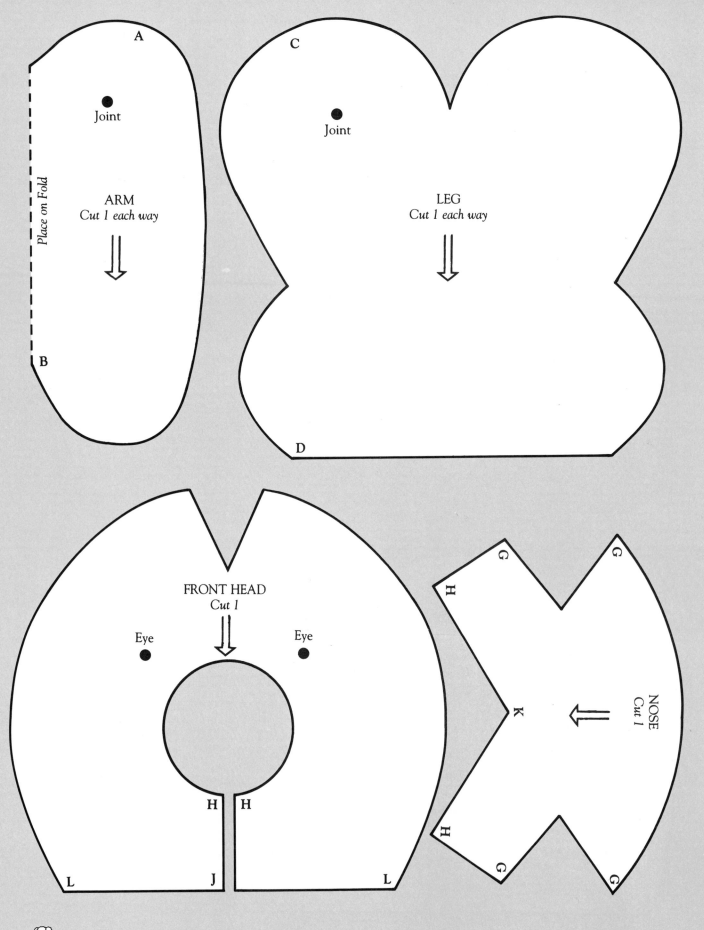

A

● Joint

ARM
Cut 1 each way
⇓

Place on Fold

B

C

● Joint

LEG
Cut 1 each way
⇓

D

FRONT HEAD
Cut 1
⇓

Eye ●   ● Eye

H H

L   J   L

G   G

H

K   **NOSE**
Cut 1
⇐

H

G   G

1 Make a pattern of each template shape (see pages 6-7) and draw around it on the wrong side of the fabric, as shown.

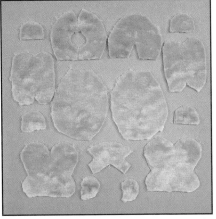

2 Cut out all the pieces and check with the picture that all the sections are there.

3 Items required: 4 joints, 4 large washers, 4 metal safety washers, 2 teddy eyes with washers, and 1 heart nose and washer.

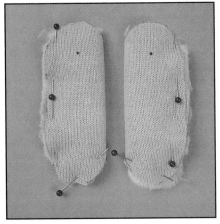

4 With right sides facing, fold the arms in half and pin from **A** to **B**.

5 Stitch along the seam lines of each arm, as shown.

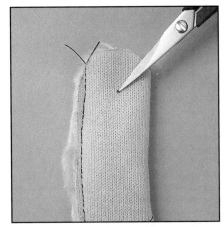

6 Cut a small hole in each arm in the position marked for the joint. Sew round hole.

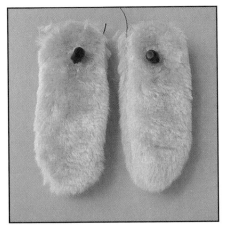

7 Turn the arms right side out and insert a small amount of filling. Insert joint through the hole in each arm (see page 9).

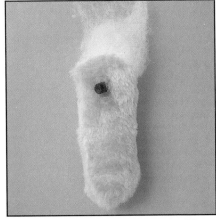

8 Stuff each arm firmly with the filling.

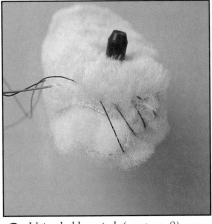

9 Using ladder stitch (see page 8), sew up the openings on each arm by hand.

10 Brush the seams on each arm. The picture shows completed arm with joint.

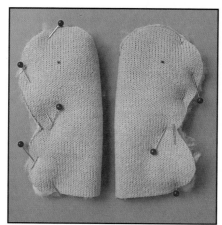

11 With right sides facing, fold the legs in half and pin from **C** to **D**.

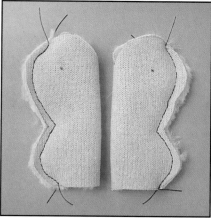

12 Stitch along the seam line on each leg, as shown.

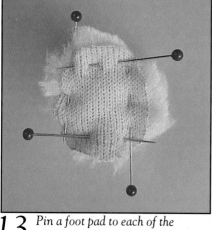

13 Pin a foot pad to each of the openings at the leg ends.

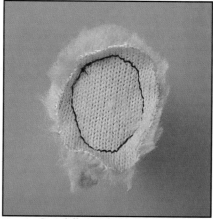

14 Carefully stitch the foot pads to the leg ends around the seam lines, making the circles as even as possible.

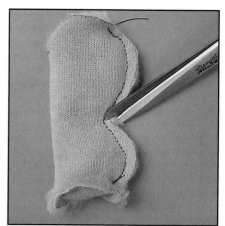

15 Snip the leg seams at the ease points and cut a small hole in each leg in the position marked for the joint. Sew round hole (see page 9).

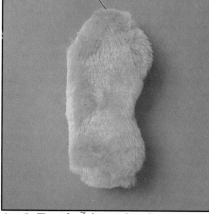

16 Turn both legs right side out.

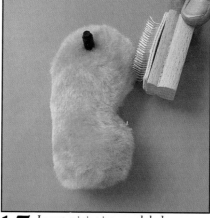

17 Insert a joint into each hole. Continue as for the arms (see steps **8-9**). Brush the seams.

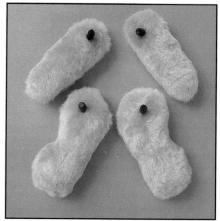

18 Picture shows the 2 completed pairs of arms and legs, with the joints in place.

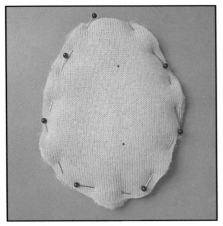

19 With right sides facing, pin the body pieces together from **E** to **F**, leaving the neck open.

20 Stitch around the body along the seam line. Cut small holes in the positions marked for the joints. Sew around holes.

21 Turn the body right side out and brush the seams.

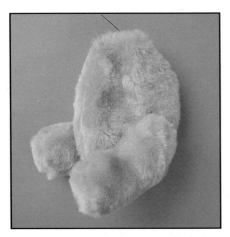

22 Insert the leg joints into the holes at the lower part of the body and fix (see page 9).

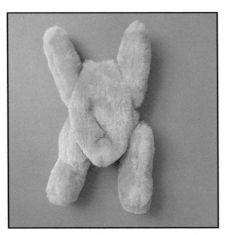

23 Repeat step *22* for the arms, inserting the joints into the holes in the upper part of the body.

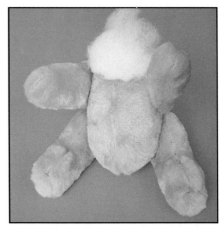

24 Stuff the body firmly with the filling.

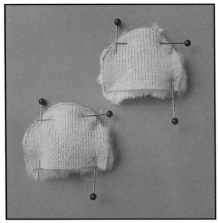

25 With right sides facing, pin the ear pieces together, as shown.

26 Stitch the ear pieces together along the seam lines, leaving the straight edges open.

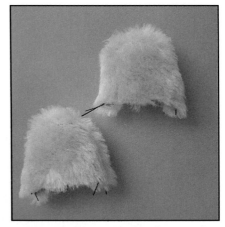

27 Turn the ears right side out and brush the seams.

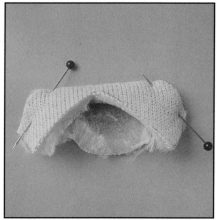

28 With right sides facing, fold the nose in half and pin the darts from **G** to **G**.

29 Stitch the darts in the nose from **G**, tapering off to nothing, as shown.

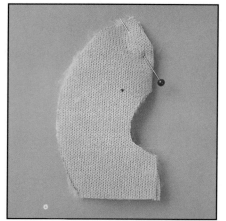

30 With right sides facing, fold the front head in half and pin the dart.

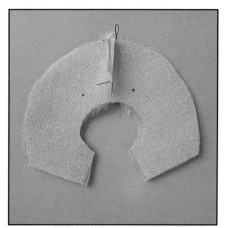

31 Stitch the dart from the outer edge, tapering off to nothing, and open out the front head piece.

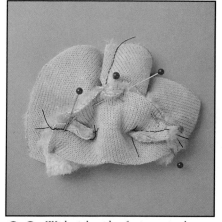

32 With right sides facing, pin the nose to the front of the head from **H** to **H**.

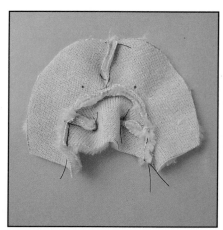

33 Carefully stitch the nose to the front head along the seam line.

34 With right sides facing, fold the front head in half and pin from **J** to **K**.

35 Stitch the nose and front head along the seam line. Insert the eyes (see page 11).

36 Insert the nose at position **K** (see page 11). Brush all the head and nose seams.

37 To complete the face, embroider a teddy mouth under the nose (see page 11).

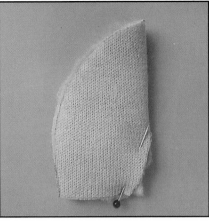

38 With right sides facing, fold the back head in half and pin the dart.

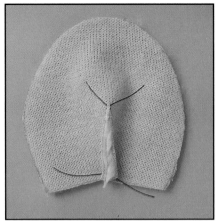

39 Stitch the dart in the back head, starting at the outer edge and tapering off to nothing.

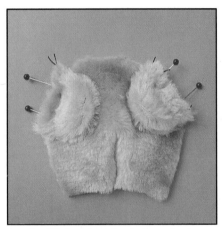

40 With right sides facing, pin the ears to either side of the back head, in the positions marked on the template.

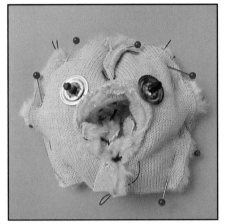

41 With right sides facing, pin the front head to the back head from **L** to **L**, leaving the neck open.

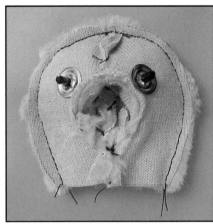

42 Stitch the front head to the back head along the seam line, as shown.

43 Turn the head right side out. Check that the ears are secured in the stitching line.

44 Stuff the head firmly with the filling.

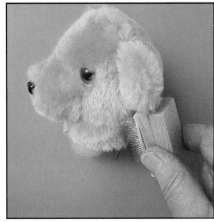

45 Brush all seams in the head.

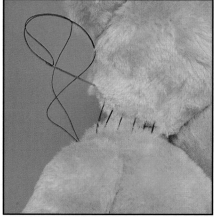

46 *Attach the head to the bear's body with ladder stitch (see page 8) and secure.*

47 *Complete the bear by tying a ribbon around its neck, securing it with a double knot.*

48 *Tie the ribbon into a bow and cut to the length required.*

TEDDY *the* GLOVE PUPPET ☆☆

MATERIALS

○ Gold Plush Fur 510mm × 355mm (20″ × 14″)
○ Honey Plush Fur 205mm × 150mm (8″ × 6″)
○ 2 Medium Teddy Eyes
○ 1 Small Animal Nose

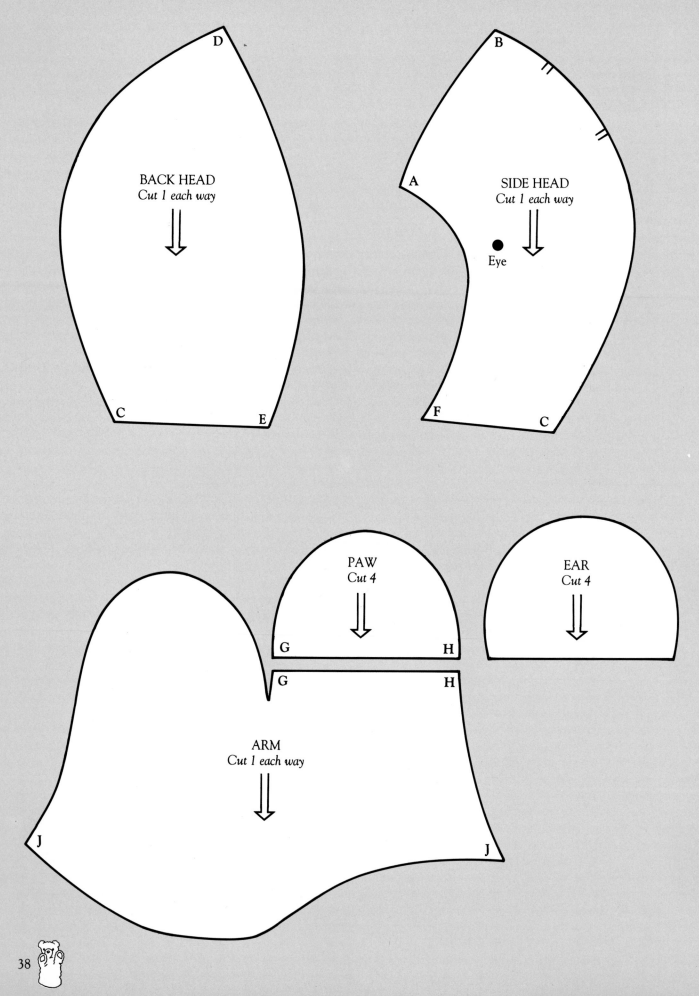

BACK HEAD
Cut 1 each way

SIDE HEAD
Cut 1 each way

Eye

PAW
Cut 4

EAR
Cut 4

ARM
Cut 1 each way

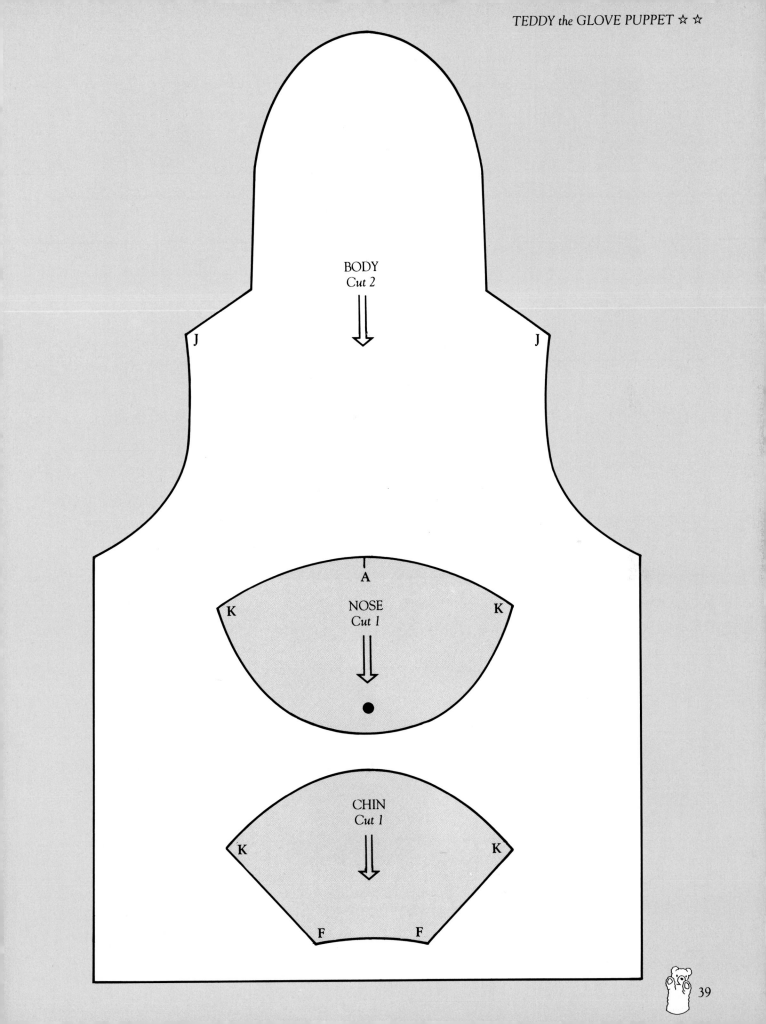

BODY
Cut 2

J   J

A

K   NOSE   K
                     Cut 1

●

CHIN
Cut 1

K   K

F   F

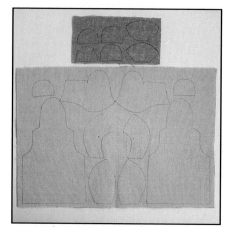

1 Make a pattern (see pages 6-7) and draw around it on the wrong side of the fabric, as shown.

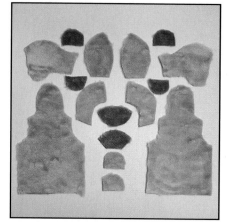

2 Cut out all the pieces and check with the picture that all the sections are there.

3 With right sides facing, pin the ear pieces together.

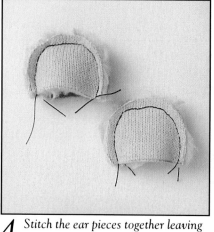

4 Stitch the ear pieces together leaving the straight edges open, as shown.

5 Turn each ear right side out and brush the seams.

6 With right sides facing, pin nose to chin from **K** to **K**.

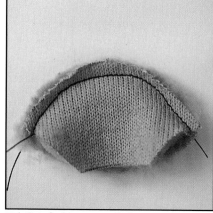

7 Stitch the nose and chin together along the seam line, as shown.

8 With right sides facing, pin back head pieces together from **D** to **E**.

9 Stitch back head pieces together along the seam line, as shown.

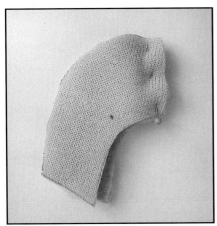

10 With right sides facing, pin side head pieces together from **A** to **B**.

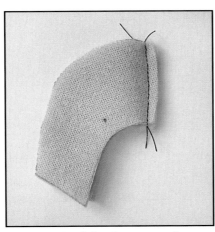

11 Stitch side head pieces together along the seam line, as shown.

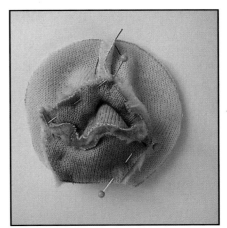

12 With right sides facing, pin the joined nose and chin to the side head from **F** to **F**.

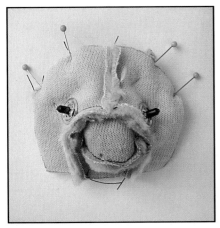

13 Stitch nose and chin to side head. Insert the eyes (see page 11). With right sides facing, pin ears to face in the positions marked on the template.

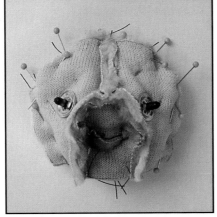

14 With right sides facing, pin the back head to the face from **C** to **C**.

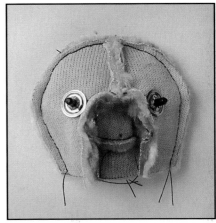

15 Stitch the back head to face from **C** to **C**, leaving the bottom edge open.

16 Turn head right side out and check that the ears are secure. Brush all seams.

17 Stuff the front of the head with filling to achieve a round, full face.

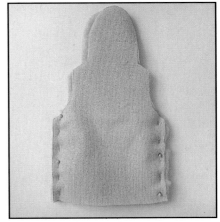

18 With right sides facing, pin body pieces together along each straight side.

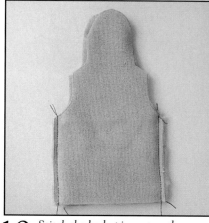

19 Stitch the body pieces together down each side, as shown.

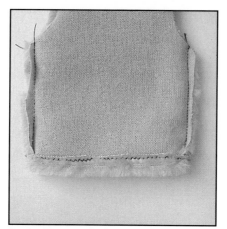

20 Turn up the bottom edge and stitch into place with a zigzag stitch.

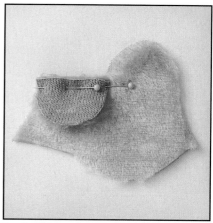

21 With right sides facing, pin a paw to an arm from **H** to **G**.

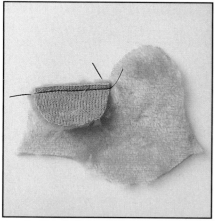

22 Stitch the paw to the arm from **G** to **H**. Repeat steps **21-22** for second paw and arm.

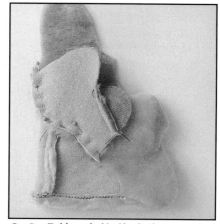

23 Fold top half of body downwards. With right sides facing, pin arm to body matching **J** to **J**.

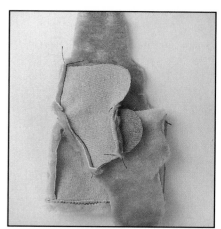

24 Stitch arm to body from **J** to **J**. Repeat steps **23-24** for second arm.

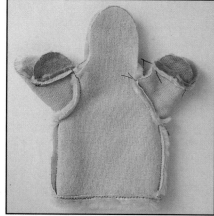

25 Fold body together and arms in half, as shown.

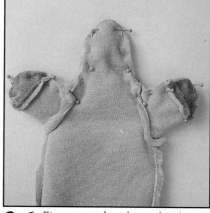

26 Pin arms and neck together from **G** to **G**, as shown.

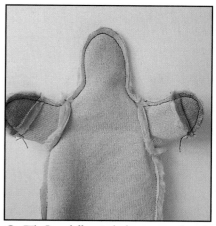

27 Carefully stitch the arms and neck together along the seam line, as shown.

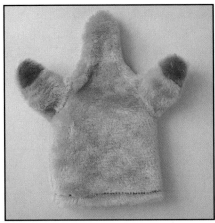

28 Turn the body right side out and brush all seams.

29 Insert neck into head, ensuring that the filling is kept to the front of the face. Position as required.

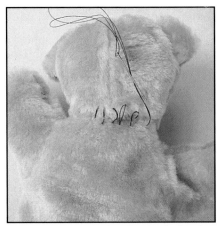

30 Keeping neck well into the head, stitch together along the neck edge with ladder stitch (see page 8) and secure. Brush the seam.

EDWARD BEAR DOORSTOP ☆☆☆☆

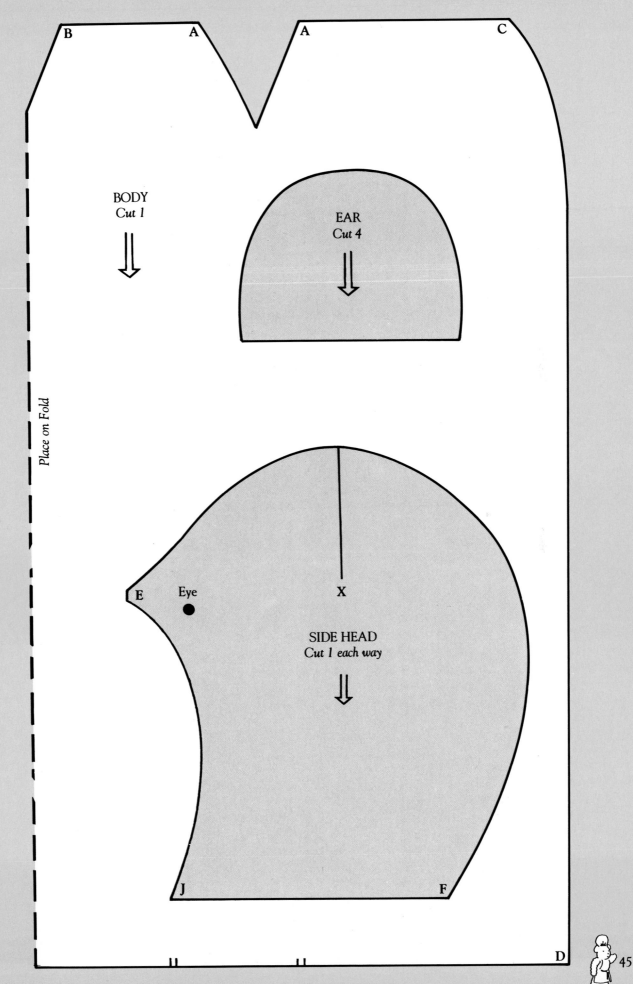

B   A   A   C

BODY
Cut 1

EAR
Cut 4

Place on Fold

E

Eye

X

SIDE HEAD
Cut 1 each way

J   F

D

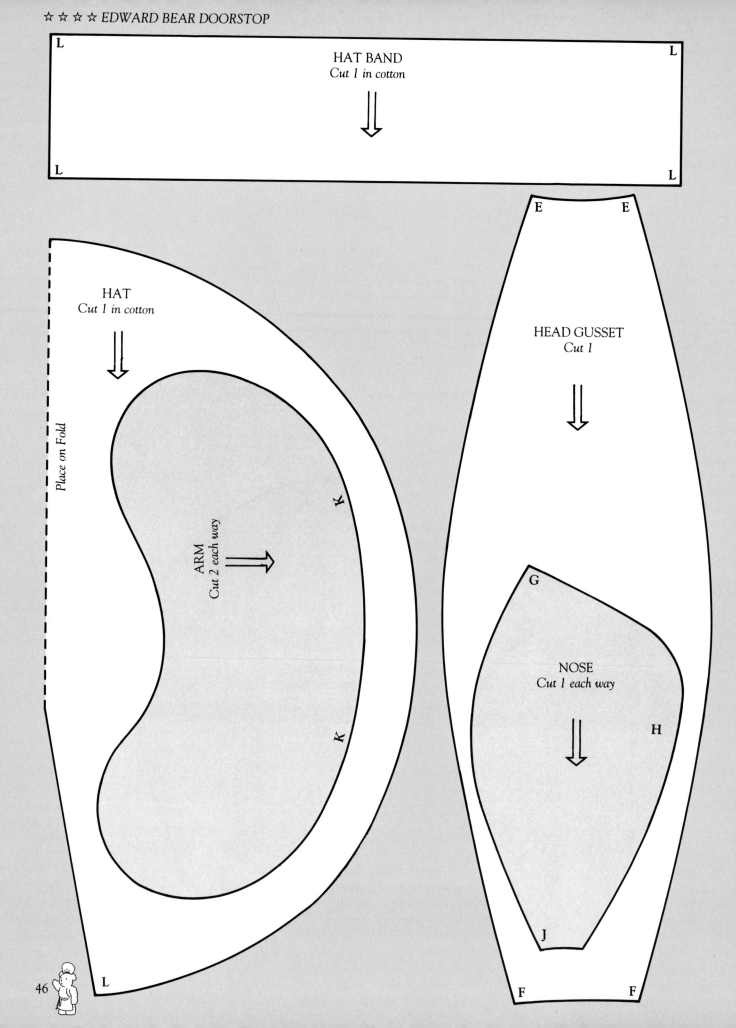

HAT BAND
Cut 1 in cotton

HAT
Cut 1 in cotton

Place on Fold

ARM
Cut 2 each way

HEAD GUSSET
Cut 1

NOSE
Cut 1 each way

46

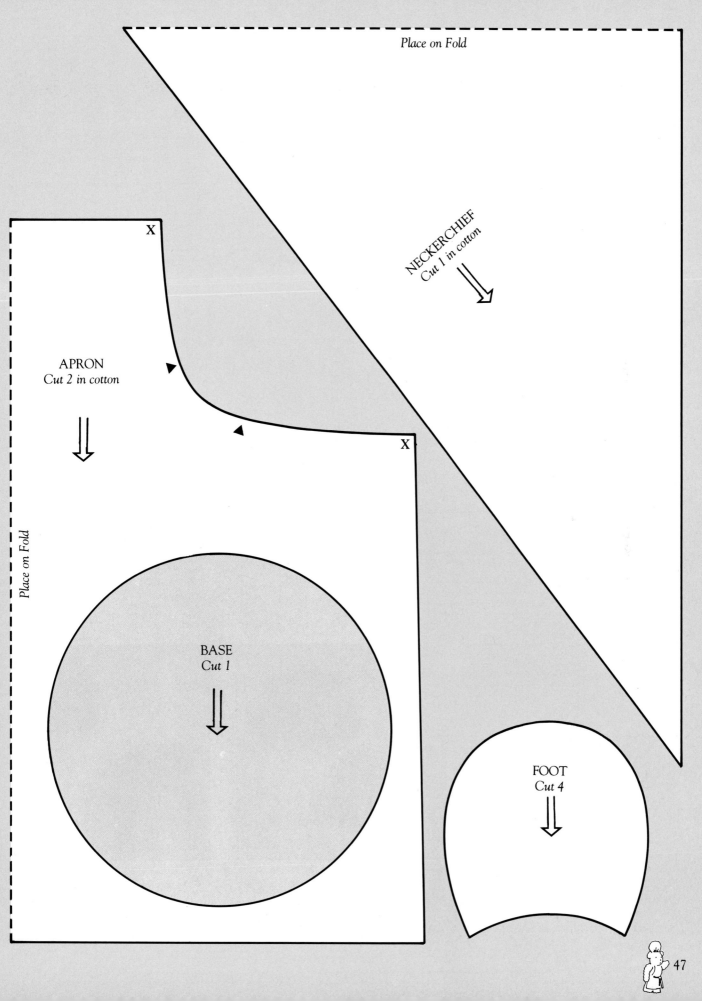

Place on Fold

NECKERCHIEF
Cut 1 in cotton

X

APRON
Cut 2 in cotton

X

Place on Fold

BASE
Cut 1

FOOT
Cut 4

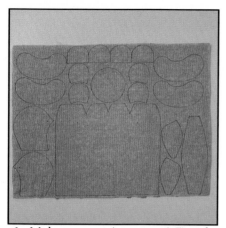

1 Make a pattern (see pages 6-7) and draw around the appropriate pieces on the wrong side of the fur fabric, as shown.

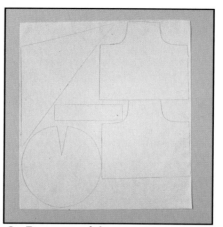

2 Draw around the appropriate pattern pieces on the wrong side of the cotton material.

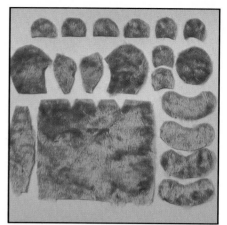

3 Cut out all the pieces from the fur fabric and check with the picture that all the sections are there.

4 Cut out all the pieces from the cotton material and check with the picture that all the sections are there.

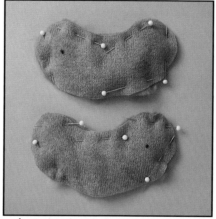

5 With right sides facing, pin the arm pieces together from **K** to **K**.

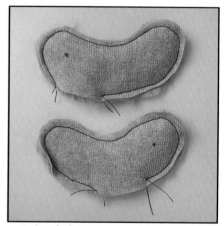

6 Stitch the arm pieces together along the seam lines, leaving an opening for turning.

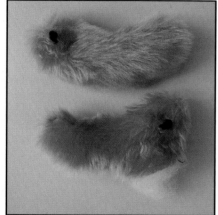

7 Cut a small hole in each arm in positions marked for the joints (see page 9). Insert a joint through the hole in each arm and stuff each arm firmly with the filling. Close with ladder stitch.

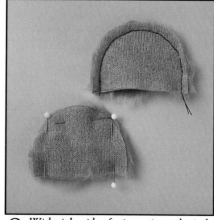

8 With right sides facing, pin and stitch the feet together, leaving the straight edges open.

9 Turn the feet right sides out, brush the seams and stuff with filling.

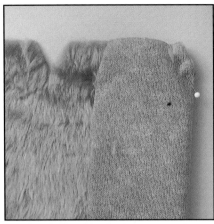

10 With right sides facing, pin the darts in the body at **A**.

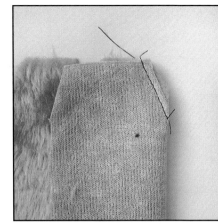

11 Stitch the darts in the body piece, as shown.

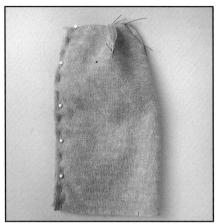

12 With right sides facing, fold the body in half lengthwise and pin from **C** to **D**.

13 Stitch the body down the side along the seam line, as shown.

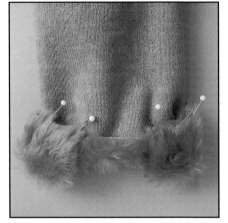

14 With right sides facing, pin the feet in the positions marked on the body template.

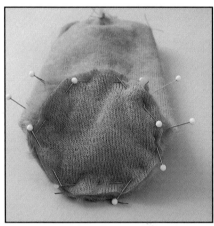

15 With right sides facing, pin the base to the body so that the feet are secured between the 2 layers of fabric.

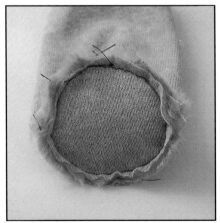

16 Stitch the base to the body. Check that the feet are well secured in the stitching line.

17 Turn the body right side out and brush all seams.

18 Cut off the top of a food tin. Wash and dry thoroughly. Put sufficient grit into a polythene bag to fill the tin.

19 *Tape up the bag of grit and place it inside the tin. Press down firmly to ensure that the tin is full.*

20 *Insert the tin through the neck of the bear's body.*

21 *Attach arms to body using joints (see page 9). Push the tin down firmly into the body.*

22 *Stuff the remaining part of the body very firmly with the filling. Brush the seams. Run a gathering stitch around the opening. Draw up the thread and secure.*

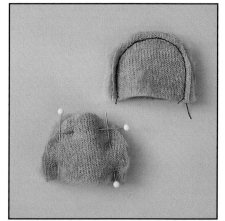

23 *With right sides facing, pin and stitch the ear pieces together, leaving the straight edges open.*

24 *Turn the ears right sides out and brush the seams.*

25 *With right sides facing, pin the head gusset to the side head from* **E** *to* **F**.

26 *Stitch the head gusset to the side head along the seam line, as shown.*

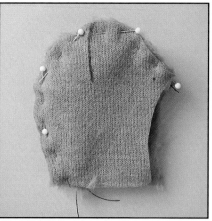

27 *With right sides facing, pin the second side head to the head gusset.*

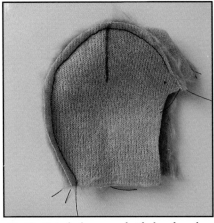

28 Stitch the second side head to the head gusset along the seam line.

29 With right sides facing, pin the nose pieces together from **G** to **H**.

30 Stitch the nose pieces together along the seam line, as shown.

31 Open out the nose. With right sides facing, pin the nose to head from **J** to **J**.

32 Stitch the nose to the head along the seam line, as shown.

33 With right sides facing, fold the nose in half and pin and stitch from **H** to neck edge.

34 Carefully cut from the bottom of mark **X** on the side head, across the top of the head, to mark on second side, as shown.

35 Insert the ears through the cut. With right sides facing, pin along cut, securing the ears between the 2 layers of fabric.

36 Stitch up the opening, tapering off at the ends. Check that the ears are secured in the stitching line.

37 Turn the head right side out and brush the seams. Insert the eyes and nose and embroider the mouth (see page 11).

38 Stuff the head with the filling until it is firm, but not too hard.

39 Run a gathering stitch around the neck. Pull up the thread slightly and secure.

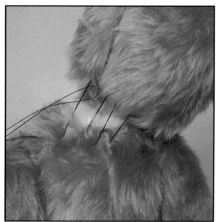

40 Attach the head to the body using a ladder stitch (see page 8) and secure. Brush the seams.

41 Run a gathering stitch around the edge of the hat from **L** to **L**.

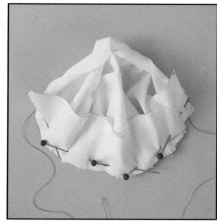

42 Draw up the gathers to fit the hat band. With right sides facing, pin and stitch the band to the hat from **L** to **L**.

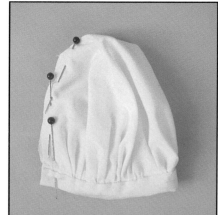

43 Press under narrow hem along edge of hat band. With wrong sides facing, fold band and slipstitch into place. With right sides facing, pin and stitch hat. Turn right side out.

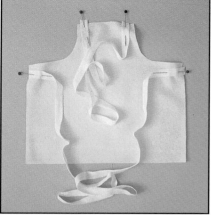

44 Cut lengths of tape for ties and pin to one of the apron pieces in the positions marked **X** on the apron template.

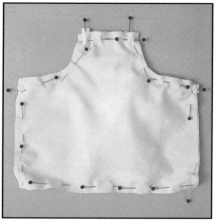

45 With right sides facing, pin and stitch the apron pieces together leaving an opening in one side for turning. Snip the seams at ease points.

46 Turn the apron right side out and stitch up the opening. Press.

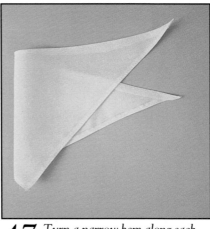

47 Turn a narrow hem along each side of the neckerchief and stitch. Press.

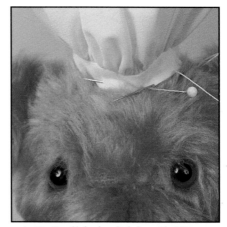

48 Stuff the hat lightly with filling. Position the hat on the bear's head and stitch into place before dressing the bear in the apron and neckerchief.

TREVOR *the* TRADITIONAL TEDDY BEAR ★★★★★

MATERIALS

○ Mohair 610mm × 455mm (24″ × 18″)
○ 2 Small Teddy Eyes
○ Black Stranded Embroidery Silk
○ Joints, 5 sets of 35mm (1½″) diameter
○ Ribbon

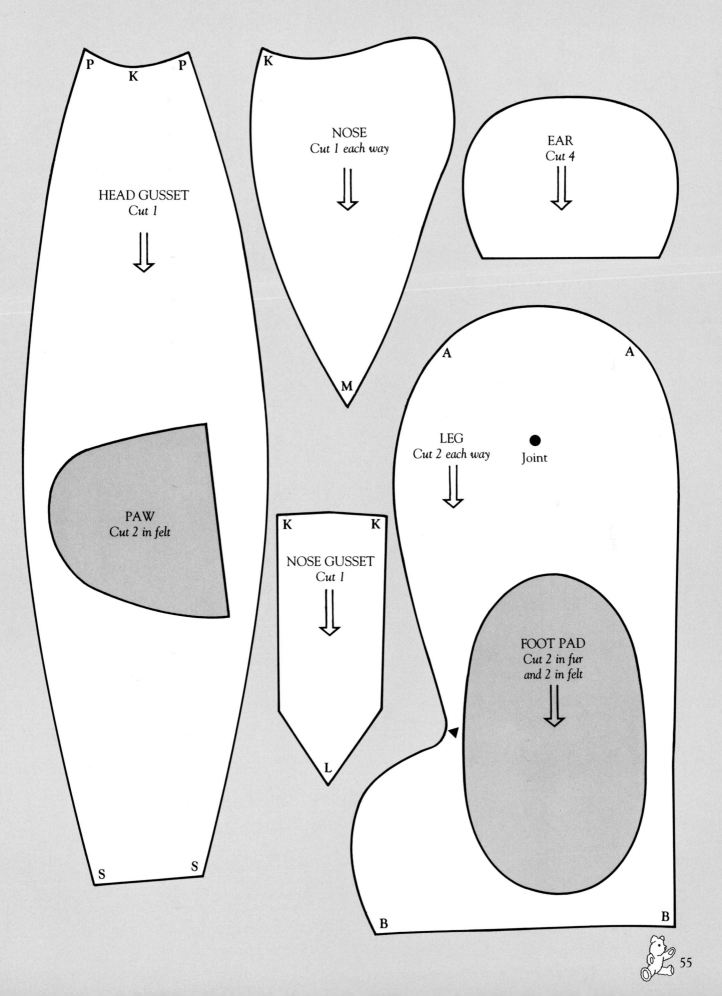

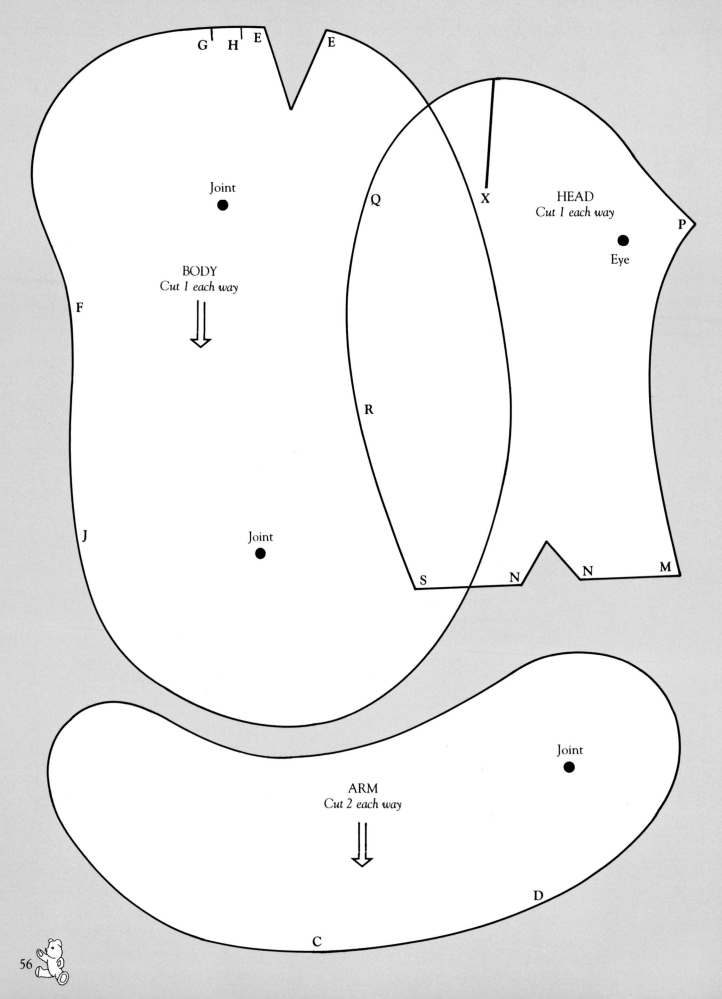

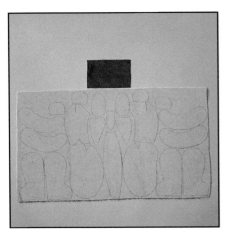

1 Make a pattern (see pages 6-7) and draw around it on the wrong side of the fabric, as shown.

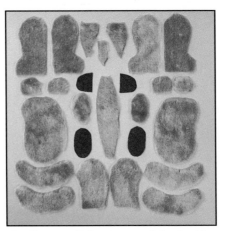

2 Cut out all the pieces and check with the picture that all the sections are there.

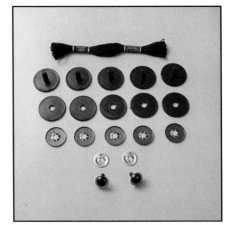

3 Items required: skein of embroidery silk, 5 joints, 5 large washers, 5 metal safety washers and 2 teddy eyes with washers.

4 Pin a felt foot pad to the right side of each fur foot pad and tack into place.

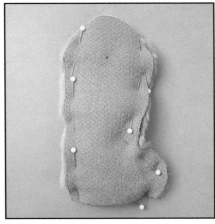

5 With right sides facing, pin 2 leg pieces together from **A** to **B** down both sides.

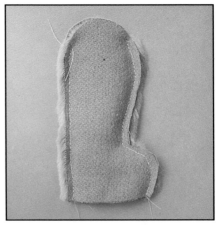

6 Stitch the leg pieces together from **A** to **B** down both sides of the leg.

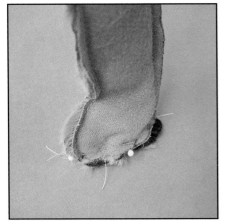

7 With the felt facing the right side of the leg, pin the foot pad to the end of the leg.

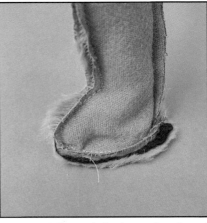

8 Carefully stitch the foot pad to the end of the leg.

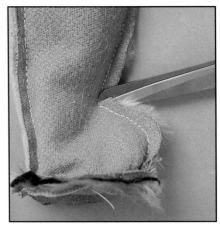

9 Snip the leg seam at the ease point. Repeat steps *4-9* for the other leg.

10 *Cut a small hole in each leg in the position marked for the joint (see page 9). Insert the joints in the right and left legs. Stuff legs firmly with filling.*

11 *Sew up the opening in the top of each leg, using ladder stitch (see page 8). Brush the seams well.*

12 *Pin a felt paw to the thin end of one arm piece, as shown.*

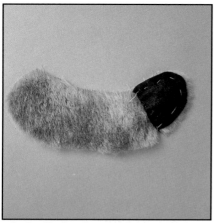

13 *Tack paw into position. With matching thread, hand stitch along the straight edge of felt paw. Repeat steps **12-13** to make one right and one left arm.*

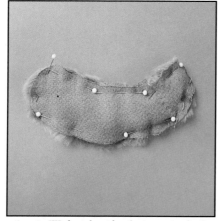

14 *With right sides facing, pin the 2 arm pieces to their corresponding outer sides.*

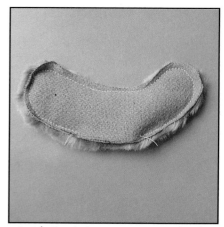

15 *Stitch the arm pieces together from **C** to **D**, leaving an opening for turning.*

16 *Turn the arms right side out and brush the seams. Insert joints in the right and left arms (see page 9) and stuff the arms firmly with the filling.*

17 *Close up arms using ladder stitch (see page 8). Brush the seams well.*

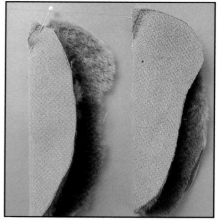

18 *With right sides facing, pin and stitch the darts in each body piece from **E**, tapering off to nothing.*

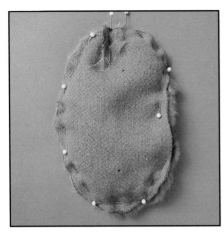

19 *With right sides facing, place the body pieces together, matching darts. Pin from **F** to **G** and **H** to **J**.*

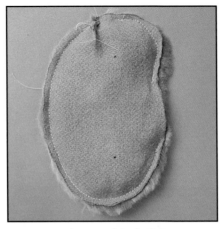

20 *Stitch around the body leaving an opening between **F** and **J**, and a small opening between **G** and **H**. Turn right side out and brush seams.*

21 *Insert limbs in positions marked on the template (see page 9), taking care that each arm and leg is facing the correct way.*

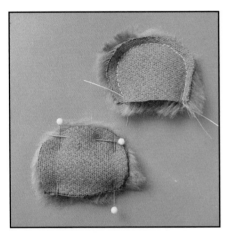

22 *With right sides facing, pin and stitch the ear pieces together, leaving the straight edges open.*

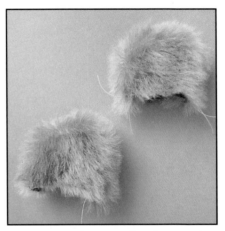

23 *Turn the ears right side out and brush the seams.*

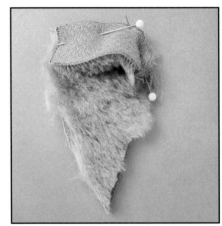

24 *With right sides facing, pin the nose gusset to one nose piece from **K** to **K** and continue round to **L**.*

25 *Stitch the nose gusset to the nose piece along the seam line, as shown.*

26 *With right sides facing, pin and stitch the second nose piece to the gusset from **K** to **M**.*

27 *With right sides facing, pin and stitch the darts in each head piece from **N** to **N**.*

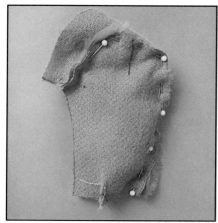

28 With right sides facing, pin the head gusset to the head from **P** to **Q** and **R** to **S**, leaving an opening between **Q** and **R**.

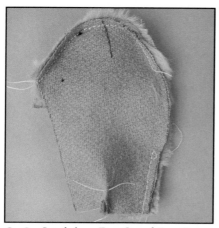

29 Stitch from **P** to **Q** and **R** to **S**. With right sides facing, pin second head piece to gusset and stitch continuously from **P** to **S**.

30 With right sides facing, pin the nose to the head from **K** to **M** and from **M** to **K**.

31 Stitch from **M** to **M**. Carefully cut from the bottom of mark **X** on the side head, across the top of the head, to mark on second side, as shown.

32 Insert the ears through the cut. With right sides facing, pin along the cut, securing the ears between the 2 layers of fabric.

33 Stitch up the opening, tapering off at the ends. Check that the ears are secured in the stitching line.

34 Turn the head right side out and brush the seams. Insert the eyes (see page 11) and embroider the nose and mouth (see page 11).

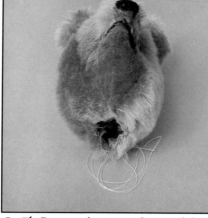

35 Run a gathering stitch around the neck opening.

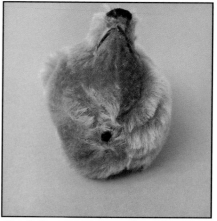

36 Insert a joint into the neck opening, leaving the peg outside. Pull up the thread tightly and secure.

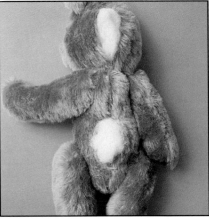

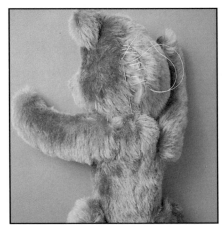

37 *Fix the head to the body by pushing the peg through the small opening in the top of the body. Secure with washers (see page 9).*

38 *Stuff the bear's body and head very firmly with the filling.*

39 *Stitch up the openings in the head and body using ladder stitch (see page 8). Brush the seams well. Complete the bear by tying a bow around its neck.*

TEDDY SHOULDER BAG ☆☆

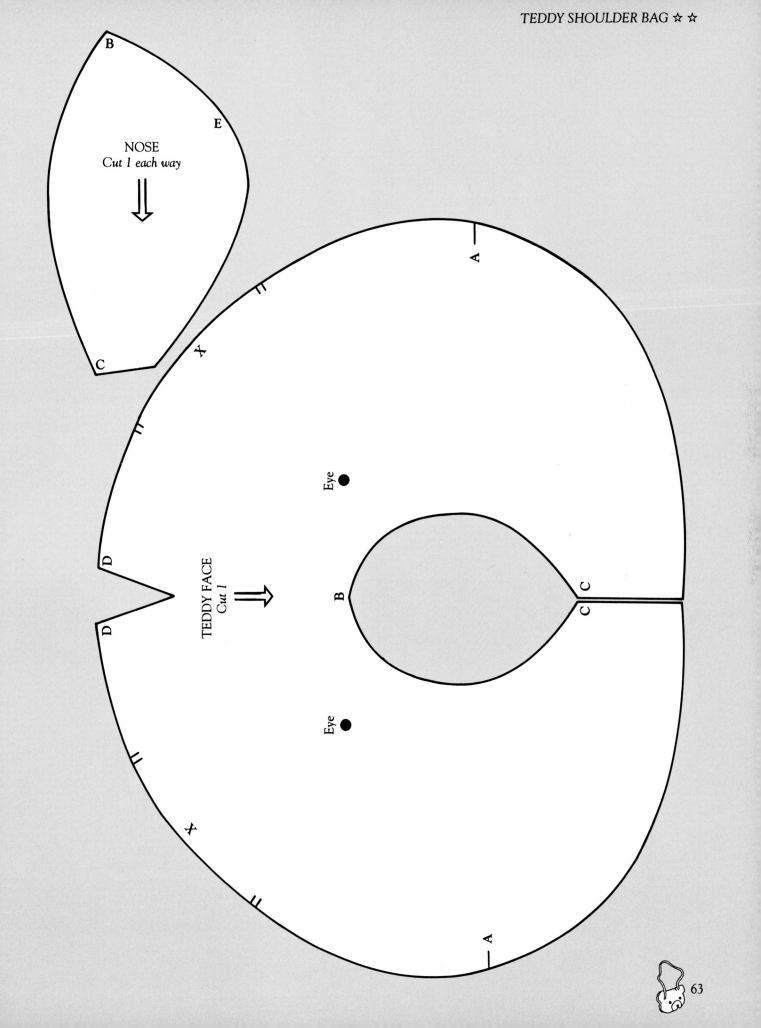

NOSE
Cut 1 each way

⇓

TEDDY FACE
Cut 1 ⇒⇒

Eye ●

Eye ●

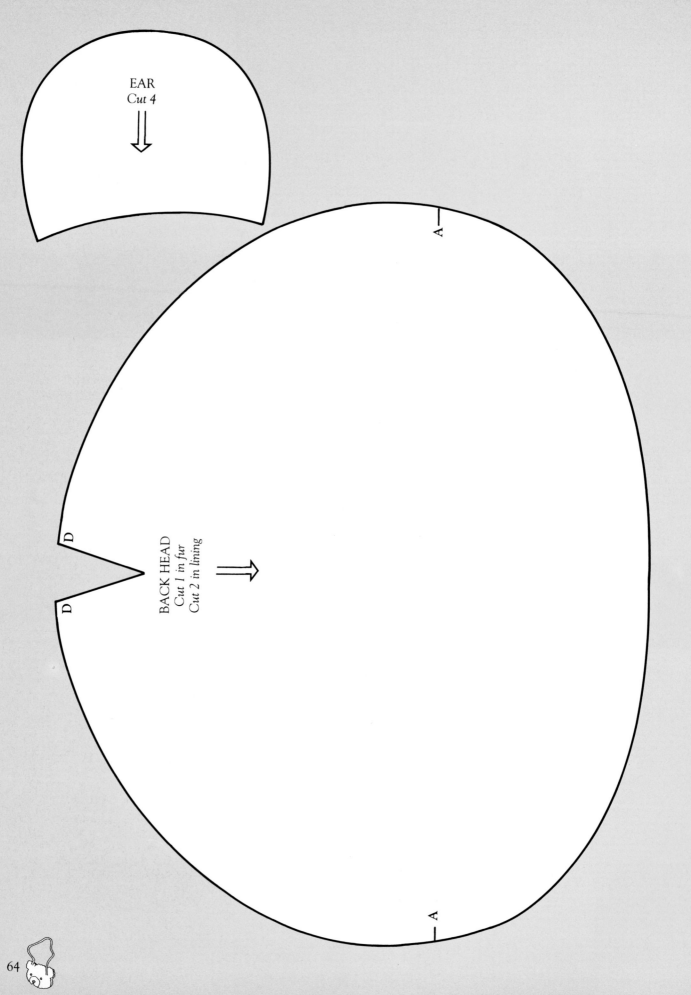

EAR
Cut 4

BACK HEAD
Cut 1 in fur
Cut 2 in lining

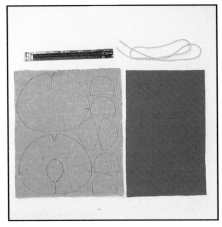

1 Make a pattern (see pages 6-7) and draw around the pieces on the wrong side of the fur fabric and lining. Items required: Zip fastener, Cord.

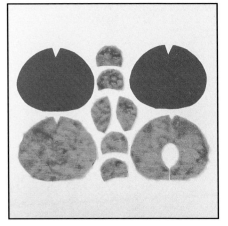

2 Cut out all the pieces and check with the picture that all the sections are there.

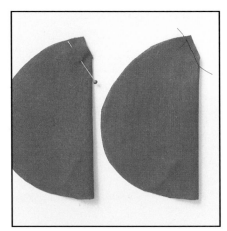

3 With right sides facing, pin and stitch the darts from **D** to **D** on the back head fur and lining pieces.

4 With right sides facing, pin the lining to the back head fur fabric along the bottom edge from **A** to **A**.

5 Stitch the lining to the back head. Snip the seam allowance at **A**.

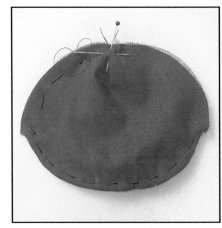

6 Turn right side out and tack from **A** all around to **A**, as shown.

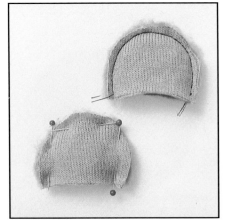

7 With right sides facing, pin and stitch the ear pieces together, leaving the straight edges open.

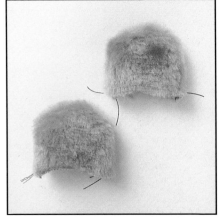

8 Turn the ears right side out and brush the seams.

9 With right sides facing, pin and stitch the nose pieces together from **B** to **E**.

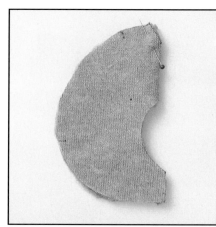

10 With right sides facing, fold the face in half and pin and stitch the dart from **D** to **D**.

11 Open out the face and, with right sides facing, pin the nose to the face, matching **B** to **C** and **C** to **B**.

12 Stitch the nose to the face along the seam line.

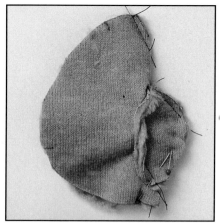

13 Fold the face in half once again, right sides facing, and pin from **E** to neck edge.

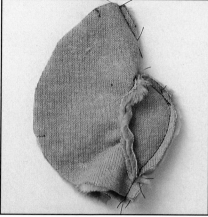

14 Stitch the remaining part of the nose along the seam line and brush the seam.

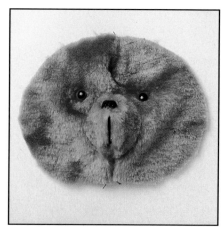

15 Insert the eyes and nose and embroider the bear's mouth (see page 11).

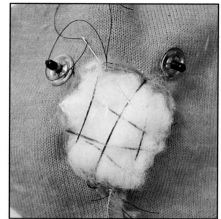

16 Stuff the nose firmly with the filling. To keep the filling in place, sew with a long thread from side to side of the nose, catching in the seam allowance.

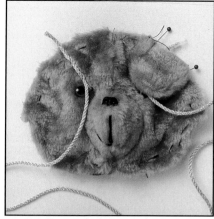

17 Secure the lining to the face. Pin the ends of the cord to the face at mark **X**. Pin ears in place, over cord, as shown.

18 With right sides facing, pin the face to the back head, matching **A** to **A**. Check that the ears are secured in the stitching line.

19 *Stitch from **A** to **A** and neaten seams with a zigzag stitch.*

20 *Turn right side out and brush the seams. Insert the zip into the opening and stitch in by hand.*

21 *Picture shows the completed shoulder bag with the zip hand-sewn into place.*

BLUE BEAR ☆☆☆☆

MATERIALS

○ Blue Polished Fur 510mm × 455mm (20″ × 18″)
○ White Polished Fur 355mm × 205mm (14″ × 8″)
○ 2 Small Teddy Eyes
○ 1 Flocked Nose
○ Ribbon 90cm × 25mm (1yd × 1″)

K

FRONT BODY
Cut 1 each way in White

⇓

L

D   D
A

HEAD GUSSET
Cut 1 in Blue

⇓

EAR
Cut 2 Blue
Cut 2 White

⇓

E   E

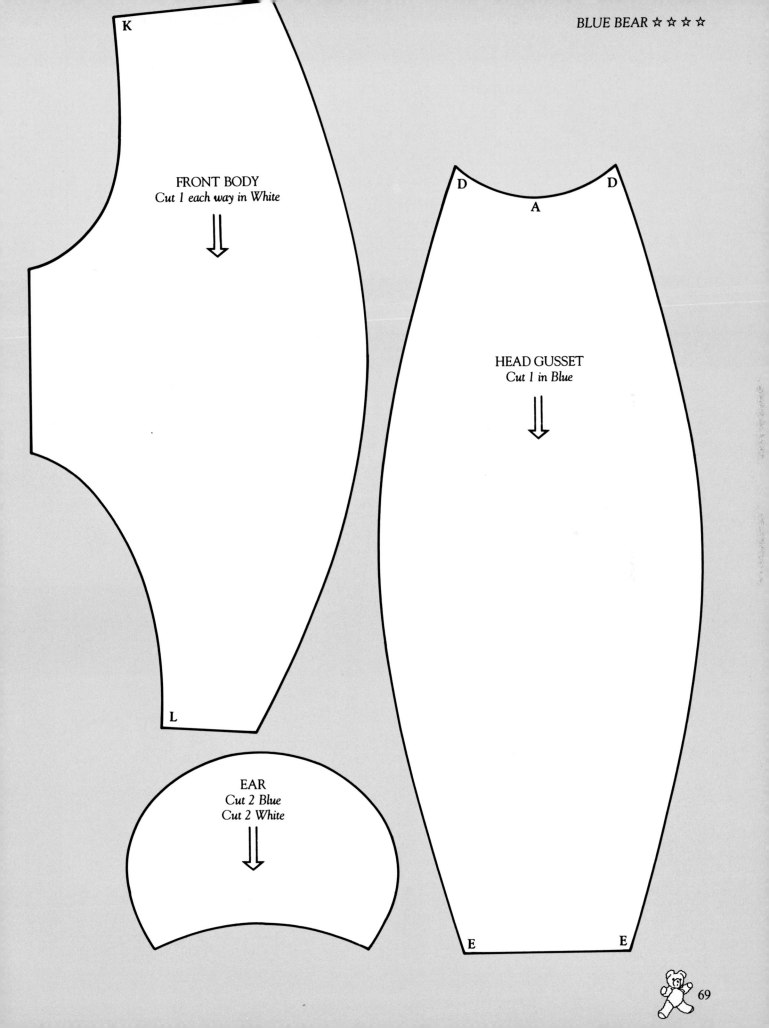

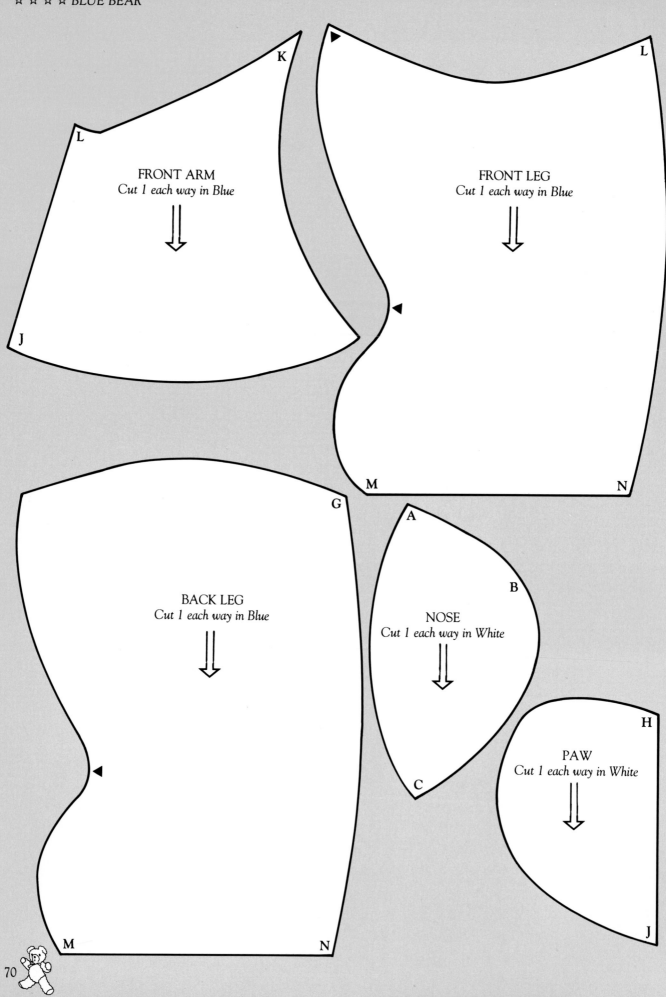

FRONT ARM
Cut 1 each way in Blue

FRONT LEG
Cut 1 each way in Blue

BACK LEG
Cut 1 each way in Blue

NOSE
Cut 1 each way in White

PAW
Cut 1 each way in White

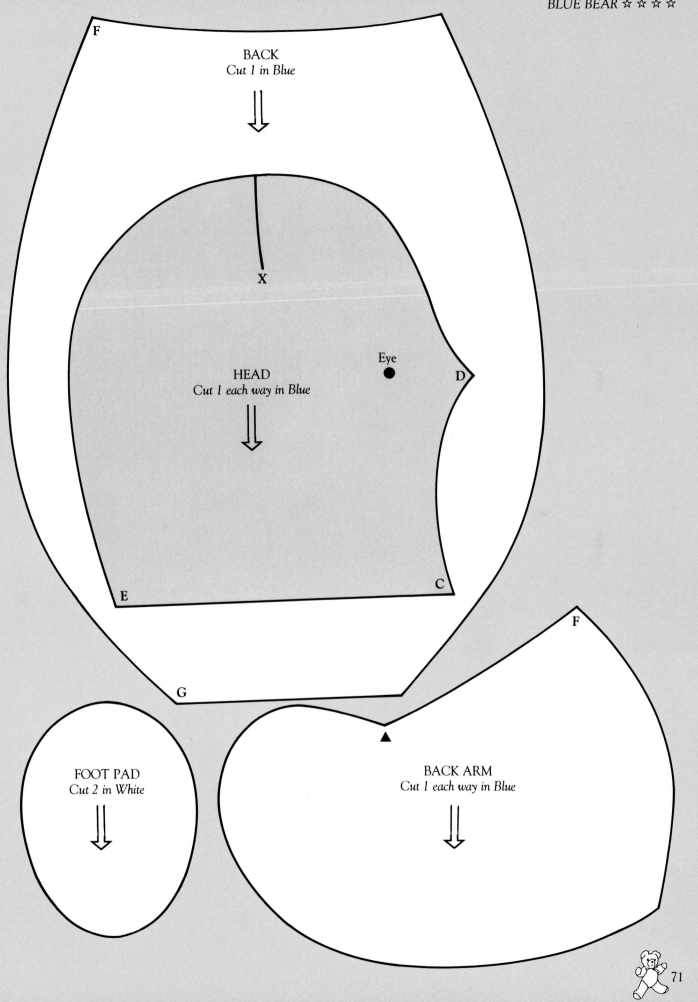

F

BACK
Cut 1 in Blue

X

Eye

D

HEAD
Cut 1 each way in Blue

C

E

G

F

FOOT PAD
Cut 2 in White

▲

BACK ARM
Cut 1 each way in Blue

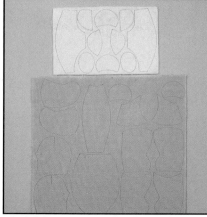

1 Make a pattern of each template shape (see pages 6-7) and draw around it on the wrong side of the fabric, as shown.

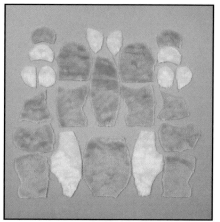

2 Cut out all the pieces and check with the picture that all the sections are there.

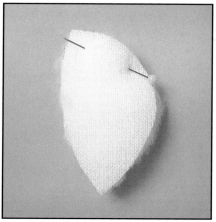

3 With right sides facing, pin the nose pieces together from **A** to **B**.

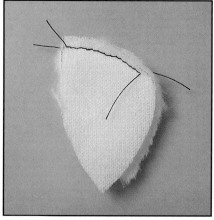

4 Stitch from **A** to **B** on the bridge of the nose, as shown.

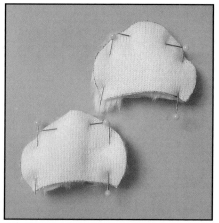

5 With right sides facing, pin the blue ear pieces to the white ear pieces.

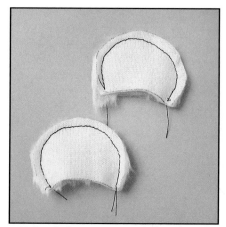

6 Stitch the ear pieces together along the seam lines, leaving the straight edges open.

7 Turn the ears right side out and brush the seams.

8 With right sides facing, pin the head gusset to one head piece from **D** to **E**.

9 Stitch the head piece to the gusset from **D** to **E**, as shown.

10 With right sides facing, pin the second side of the head to the head gusset from **D** to **E**.

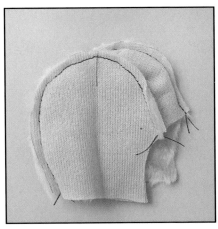

11 Carefully stitch along the seam line from **D** to **E**, as shown.

12 Carefully cut from the bottom of mark **X** on the side head, across the top of the head, to mark on second side, as shown.

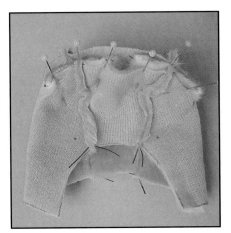

13 With the white side of the ears facing the front, insert the ears through the cut. Position and pin the ears between the 2 layers.

14 With right sides facing, pin along the cut between **X** and **X**, securing the ears between the 2 layers of fabric.

15 Stitch up the opening, tapering off at the ends. Check that the ears are secured in the stitching line.

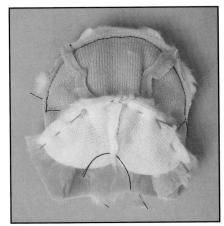

16 With right sides facing, pin the nose to the head from **C** to **C**, matching at **A**.

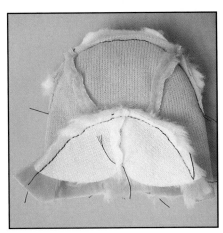

17 Stitch the nose into position along the seam line, as shown.

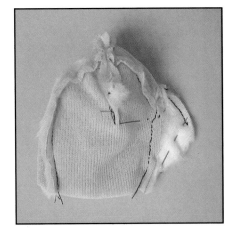

18 With right sides facing, fold the nose in half, and pin along the open edge.

73

19 Stitch the remaining part of the nose and insert the eyes in the position shown (see page 11).

20 Insert the nose, and embroider a teddy mouth (see page 11).

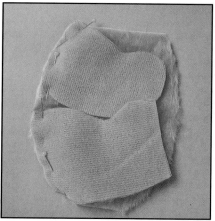

21 With right sides facing, pin one back arm to back, starting at **F**. Again with right sides facing, pin one back leg to the back, starting at **G**.

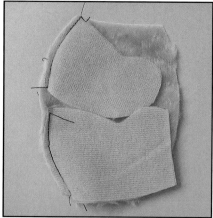

22 Following the seam line, stitch the back arm and back leg to the back of the body. Repeat for the second arm and leg.

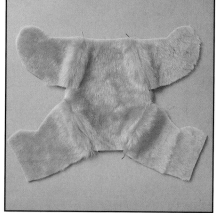

23 Open out the back pieces and brush all the seams.

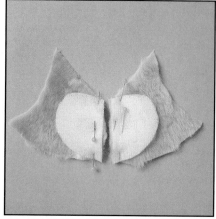

24 With right sides facing, pin the paws to the front arms, matching **H** to **J**.

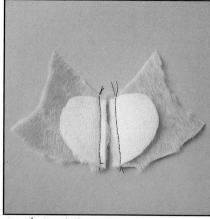

25 Stitch the paws to the front arms along the seam line.

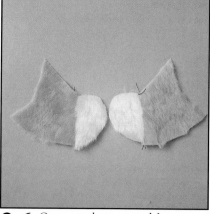

26 Open out the paws and front arms and brush the seams.

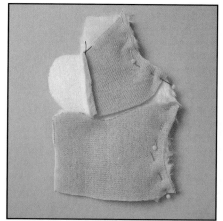

27 With right sides facing, pin one front arm to one half of the front body, starting at **K**. Pin one front leg to the front body half starting at **L**.

28 *Following the seam lines, stitch the front arm and leg to the front body half. Repeat for the second arm and leg.*

29 *With right sides facing, place the 2 front halves together and pin down the centre seam.*

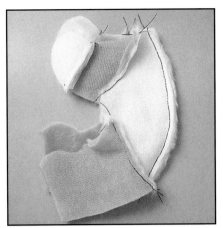

30 *Stitch the 2 front halves together along the seam line.*

31 *Open out the front pieces and brush all the seams.*

32 *With right sides facing, place the front onto the back. Pin from the top of the arm to **M**, **N** to **N** on the second leg, and from **M** to the top of the arm.*

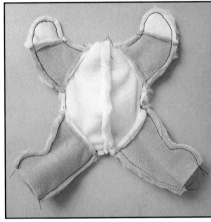

33 *Stitch along the seam lines, leaving the feet and neck open, as shown.*

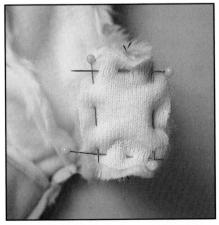

34 *Pin a foot pad to each of the leg openings.*

35 *Carefully stitch the foot pads to the leg ends around the seam lines, making the circles as even as possible.*

36 *Snip the seams at the ease points and turn the bear right side out.*

37 Brush all the seams.

38 Stuff the head and body with the filling until firm, but not too hard.

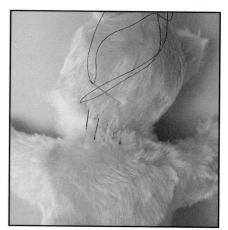

39 Hand sew the body to the head with ladder stitch (see page 8). Complete the bear by tying a bow of ribbon around its neck, securing it with a double knot.

GERALD the HOT TEDDY ☆☆☆

MATERIALS

○ Honey Polished Fur 610mm × 510mm (24″ × 20″)
○ Red Polished Fur 305mm × 404mm (12″ × 16″)
○ Cotton Lining 205mm × 205mm (8″ × 8″)
○ 2 Small Teddy Eyes
○ 1 Flocked Nose

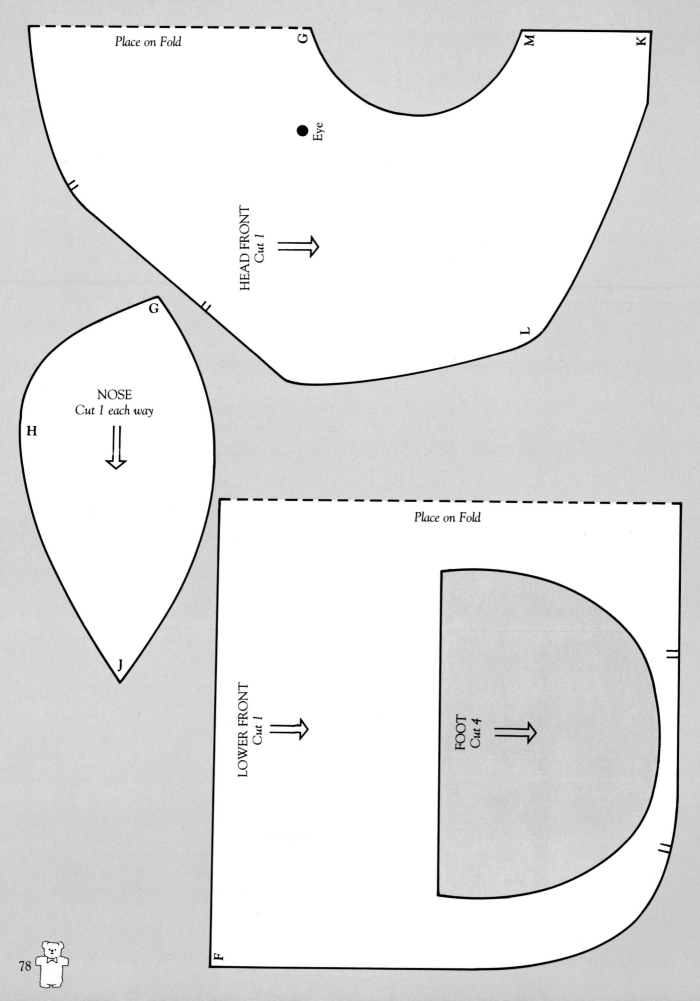

Place on Fold

G

M

K

● Eye

HEAD FRONT
Cut 1 ⇒

L

G

NOSE
Cut 1 each way
⇓

H

J

Place on Fold

LOWER FRONT
Cut 1 ⇒

FOOT
Cut 4 ⇒

F

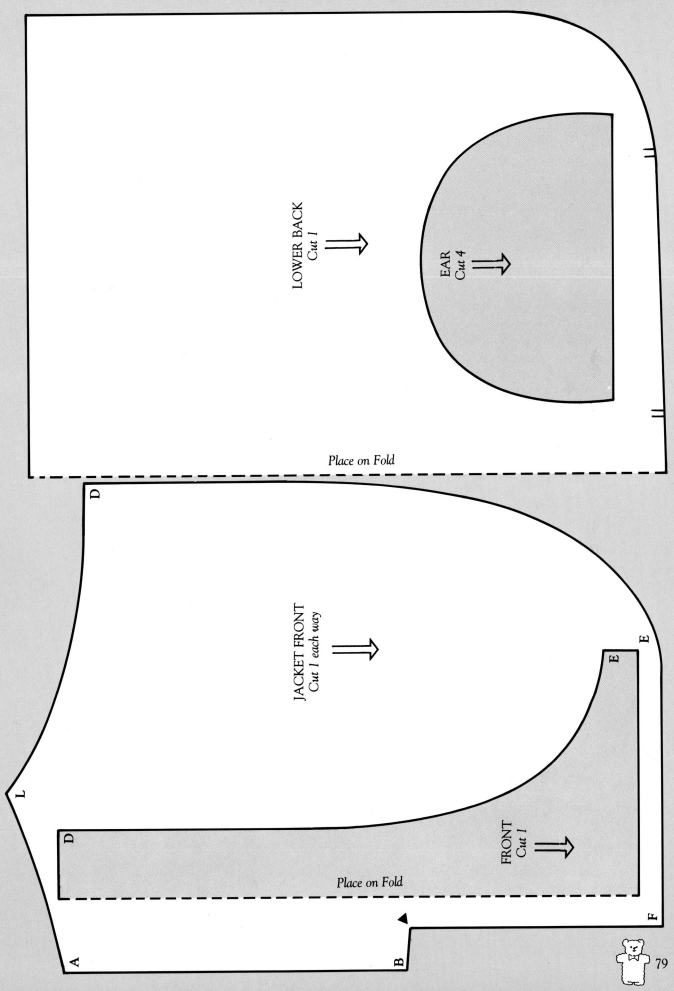

LOWER BACK
Cut 1 ⟹

EAR
Cut 4 ⟹

Place on Fold

D

JACKET FRONT
Cut 1 each way ⟹

L

D

E

E

FRONT
Cut 1 ⟹

Place on Fold

A

B

F

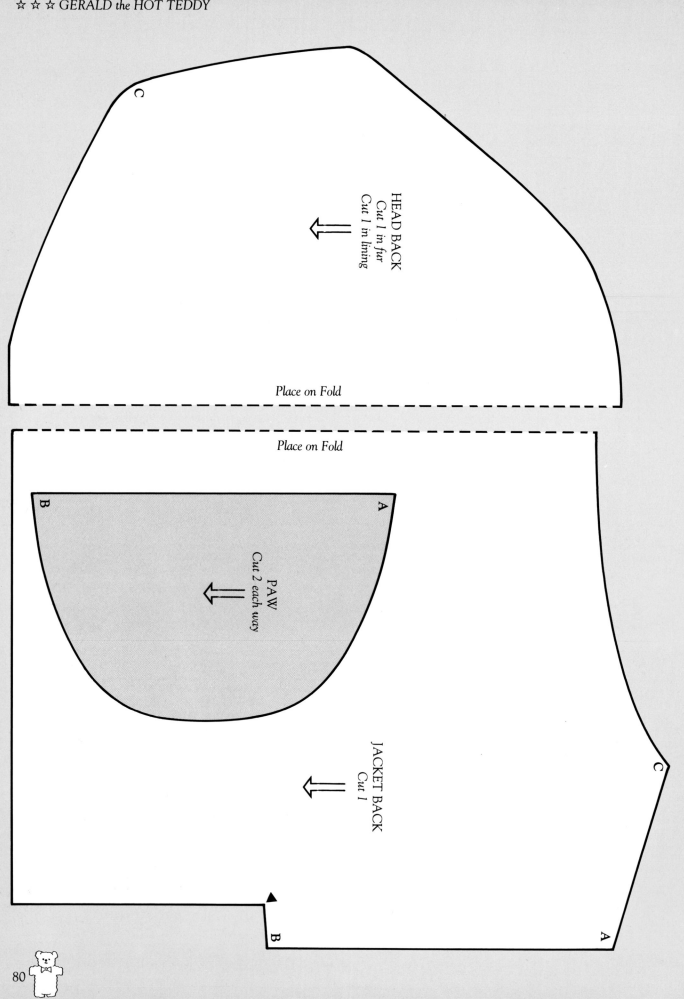

C

HEAD BACK
Cut 1 in fur
Cut 1 in lining

Place on Fold

Place on Fold

B

A

PAW
Cut 2 each way

JACKET BACK
Cut 1

C

▲

B

A

1 Make a pattern (see pages 6-7) and draw around the appropriate pieces on the wrong side of the fur fabric, as shown.

2 Draw around the appropriate pattern pieces on the wrong side of the jacket fabric. Cut the head lining from cotton fabric.

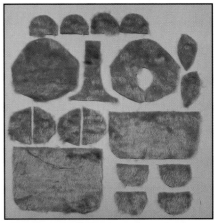

3 Cut out all the pieces from the fur fabric and check with the picture that all the sections are there.

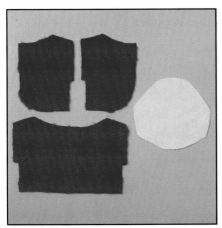

4 Cut out the jacket pieces and the cotton lining facing. Check with the picture that all the pieces are there.

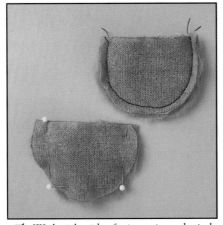

5 With right sides facing, pin and stitch the foot pieces together, leaving the straight edges open.

6 Turn the feet right side out and brush the seams.

7 To make a hem along the bottom edge of the jacket and lower back, turn the seam allowances to the wrong side and secure with a zigzag stitch.

8 Pin and stitch 2 of the paws between **A** and **B** on either side of the jacket back.

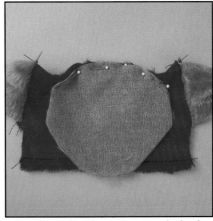

9 With right sides facing, pin the back head to jacket back, matching **C** to **C**.

10 Stitch the back head to the jacket back along the seam line.

11 Pin the remaining 2 paws between **A** and **B** on each front jacket piece.

12 Stitch the paws to the front jacket pieces along the seam lines.

13 With right sides facing, pin the front to one front jacket piece from **D** to **E**, as shown.

14 Stitch the front to the jacket front piece along the seam line and brush the seam.

15 With right sides facing, pin the second jacket front to the front, from **D** to **E**.

16 Stitch the second jacket front to the front along the seam line and brush the seam.

17 With right sides facing, pin the lower front along the lower edge of the front and front jacket pieces, matching **F** to **F**.

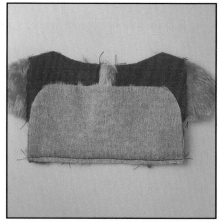

18 Stitch the lower front to the front and jacket pieces along the seam line and brush the seam.

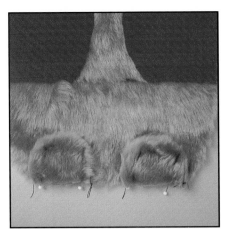

19 With right sides facing, pin the feet to the lower front in the positions marked on the template.

20 With right sides facing, pin and stitch the ear pieces together, leaving the straight edges open.

21 Turn the ears right side out and brush the seams.

22 With right sides facing, pin the nose pieces together from **H** to **H**.

23 Stitch the nose pieces together along the seam line, and brush the seam.

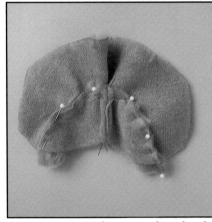

24 Open out the nose and, with right sides facing, pin it to the head from **G** to **J** and **J** to **G**.

25 Stitch the nose to the head along the seam line and brush the seam.

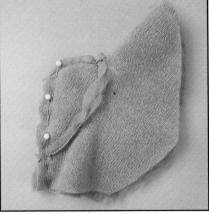

26 With right sides facing, fold the head in half and pin the nose from **H**, matching **J** to **K**.

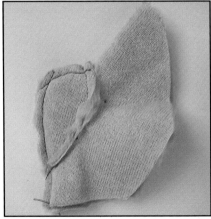

27 Stitch the remaining part of the nose along the seam line and brush the seam.

28 Brush all the seams. Insert the eyes and nose, and embroider the mouth (see page 11).

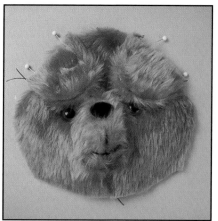

29 Pin the ears to the head front in the positions marked on the template.

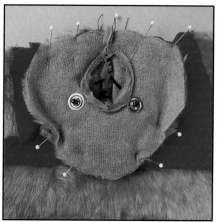

30 With right sides facing, pin the front head to the front body, matching **L** to **L**.

31 Turn the body over. Pin the cotton lining to the front from **L** to **L**, catching in the body between the 2 head layers, as shown.

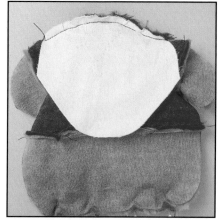

32 Stitch the cotton head lining to the front along the seam line. Check that the body is secured in the stitching line. Brush the seam.

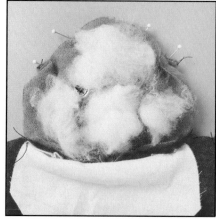

33 Stuff the nose, and lightly stuff the front of the face, with the filling.

34 Fold the cotton lining over the back of the face and pin it into position.

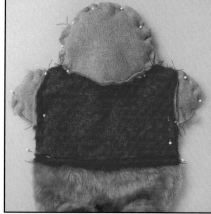

35 With right sides facing, pin the jacket back over the front body, as shown.

36 With right sides facing, pin the lower back over the front. Keep the bottom edges even so that it overlaps the jacket back.

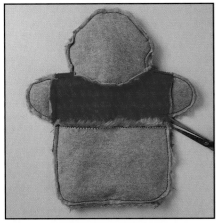

37 *Stitch around the whole body. Snip the seams at the ease points.*

38 *Turn the teddy right side out and brush the seams.*

39 *Insert a hot water bottle through the opening in the back. Complete the teddy by attaching a bow of ribbon to its neck.*

MILLIE *the* MODERN TED ☆☆☆

MATERIALS

○ Plush Fur 710mm × 610mm (28″ × 24″)
○ Pink Plush Fur 205mm × 130mm (8″ × 5″)
○ 1 Large Heart Nose
○ Black Stranded Embroidery Silk

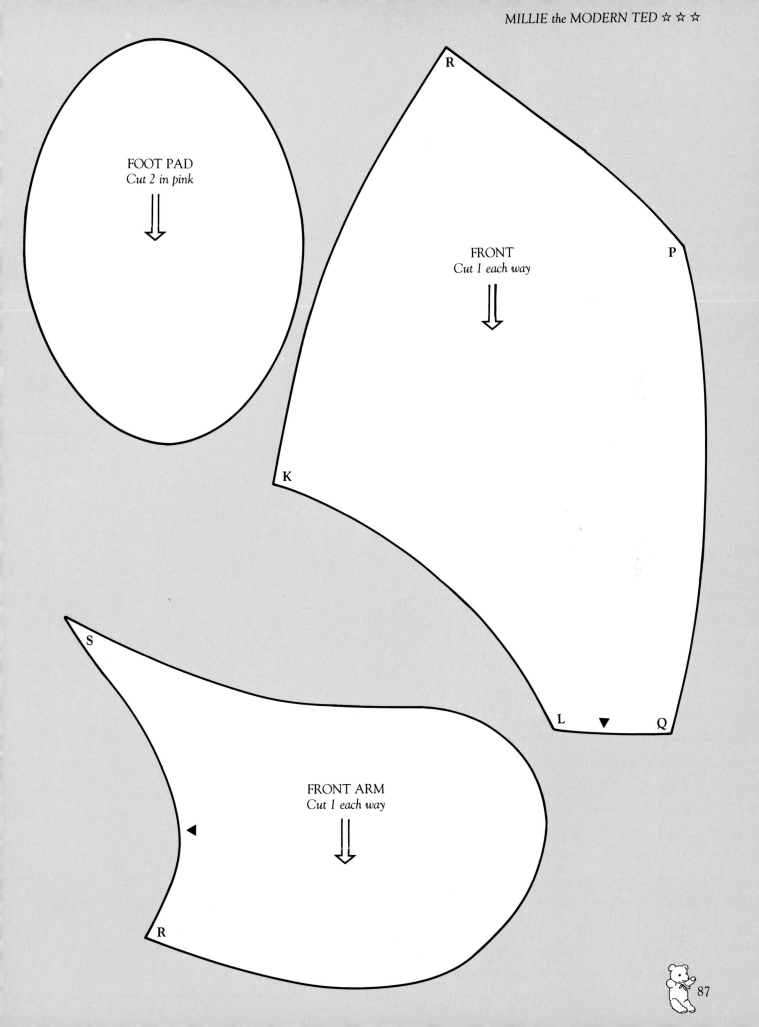

FOOT PAD
Cut 2 in pink

FRONT
Cut 1 each way

FRONT ARM
Cut 1 each way

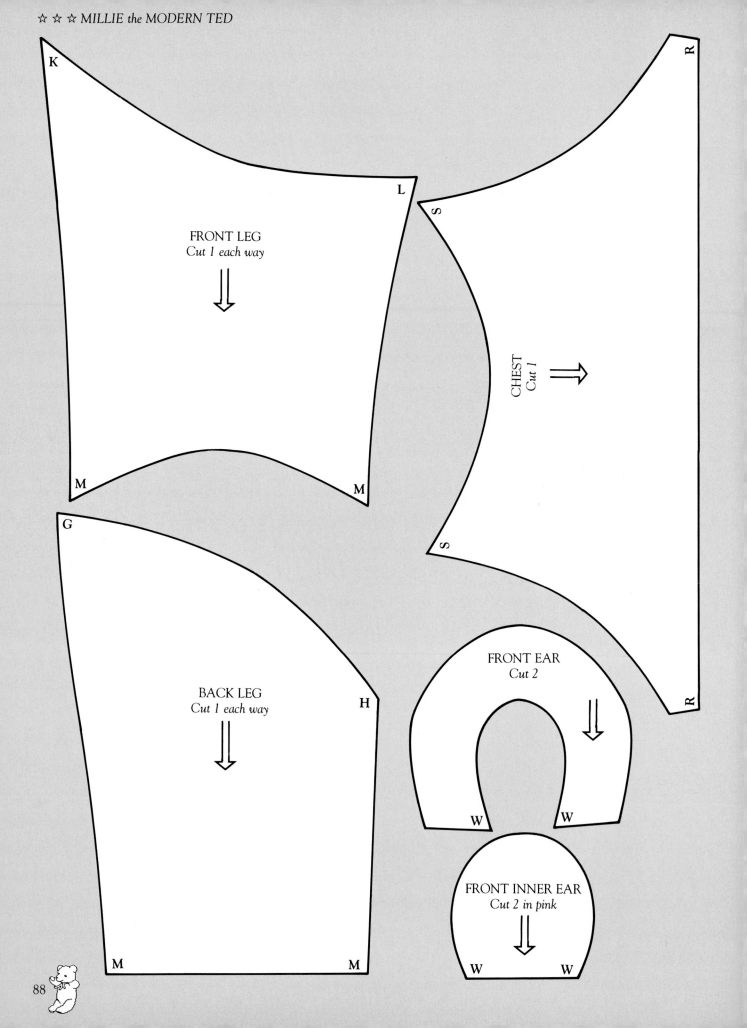

K

FRONT LEG
Cut 1 each way
⇓

L

S

R

CHEST
Cut 1 ⇒

M   M

S

G

BACK LEG
Cut 1 each way
⇓

H

FRONT EAR
Cut 2
⇓

R

M   M

W   W

FRONT INNER EAR
Cut 2 in pink
⇓

W   W

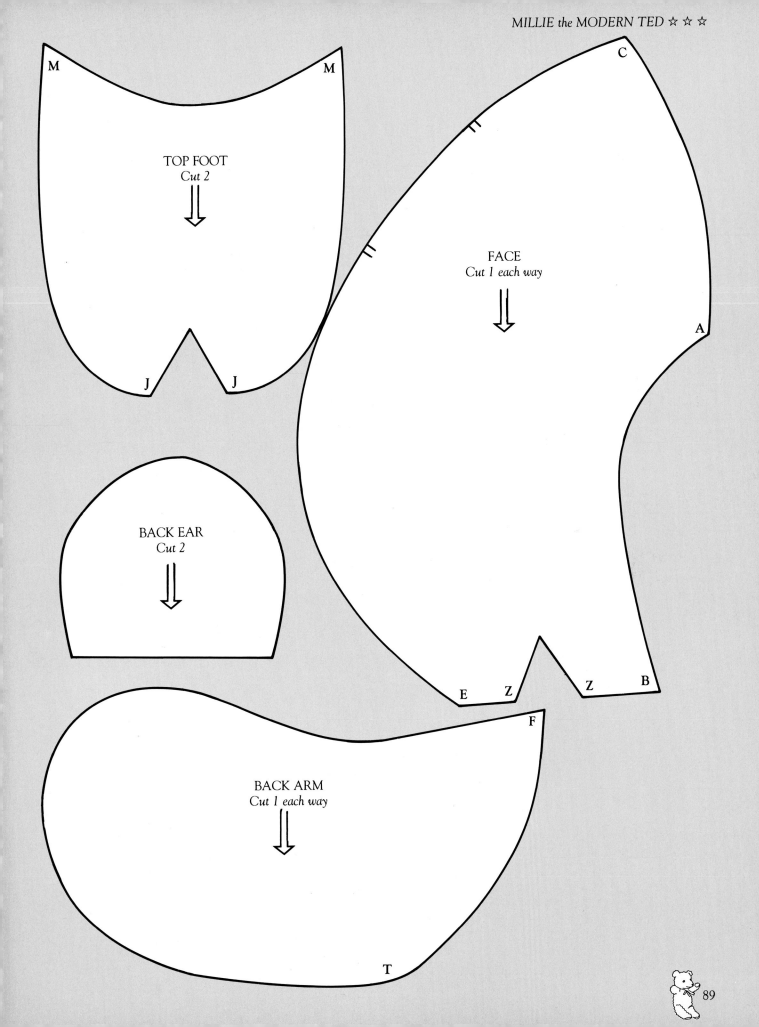

TOP FOOT
Cut 2

FACE
Cut 1 each way

BACK EAR
Cut 2

BACK ARM
Cut 1 each way

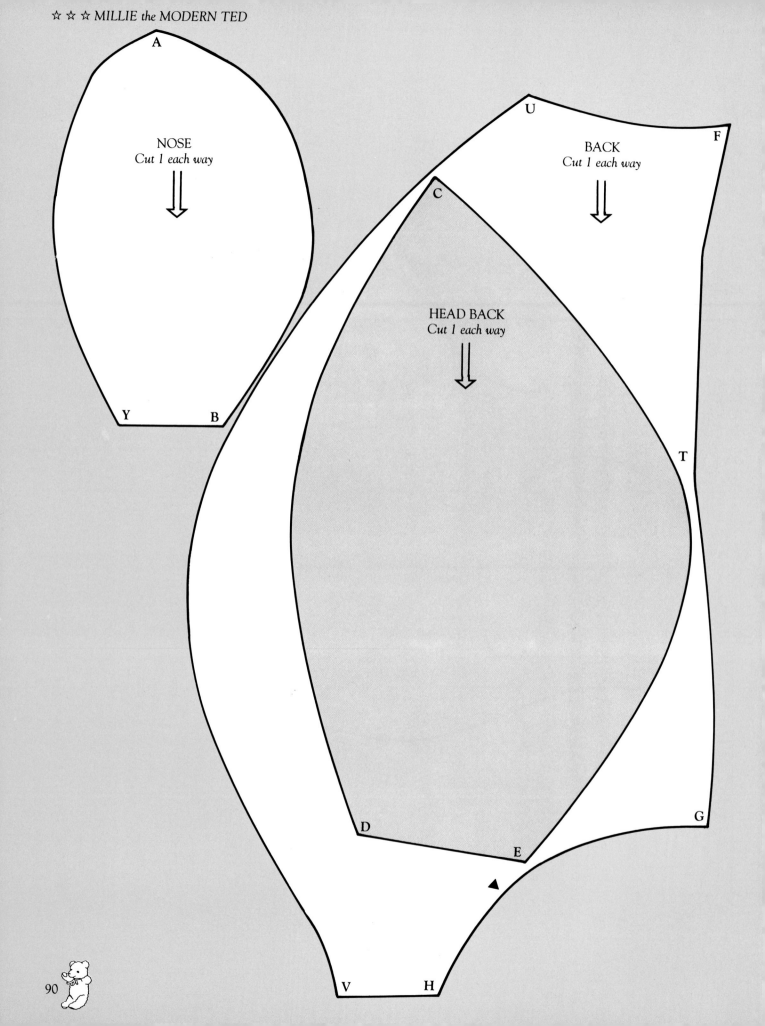

NOSE
Cut 1 each way

⇓

A

Y   B

BACK
Cut 1 each way

⇓

U   F

C

HEAD BACK
Cut 1 each way

⇓

T

D   E   G

V   H

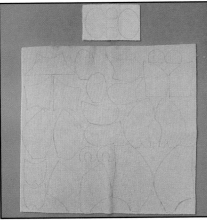

1 Make a pattern (see pages 6-7) and draw around the appropriate pieces on the wrong side of the fur fabric. Draw the foot pads and front inner ears on the pink fabric.

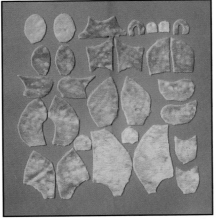

2 Cut out all the pieces and check with the picture that all the sections are there.

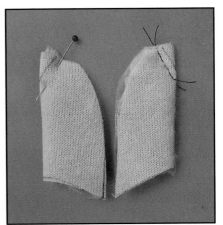

3 With right sides together, pin and stitch the darts in the bottom of the front feet, matching **J** to **J**.

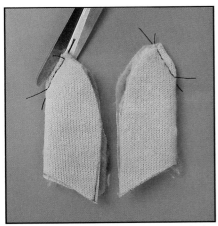

4 Trim the excess fabric from the darts, as shown.

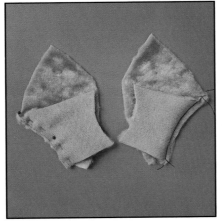

5 With right sides facing, pin and stitch the front legs to the front from **K** to **L**.

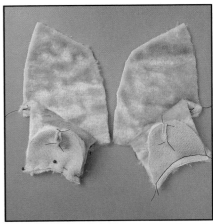

6 With right sides facing, pin and stitch the top feet to the front legs from **M** to **M**, as shown.

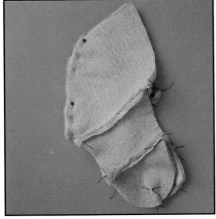

7 With right sides facing, pin the front body pieces together from **P** to **Q**.

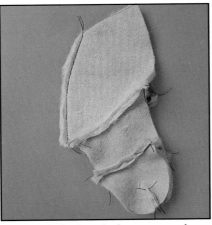

8 Stitch the front body pieces together along the seam line and brush the seam.

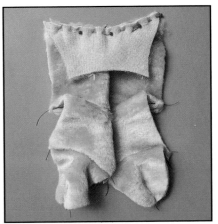

9 With right sides facing, pin the chest to the body front from **R** to **R**.

10 Stitch the chest to the front body along the seam line and brush the seam.

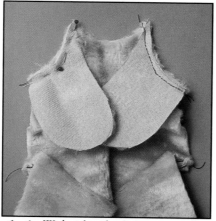

11 With right sides facing, pin and stitch the front arm pieces to the front body from **R** to **S**. Brush the seams.

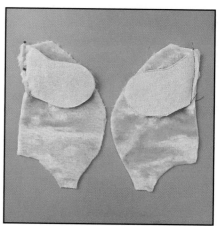

12 With right sides facing, pin and stitch the back arm pieces to the back body pieces from **F** to **T**. Brush the seams.

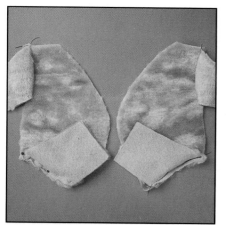

13 With right sides facing, pin and stitch the back leg pieces to the back body pieces from **G** to **H**. Brush the seams.

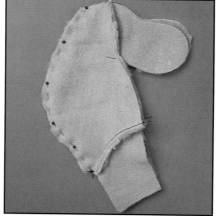

14 With right sides facing, pin the back body pieces together from **U** to **V**.

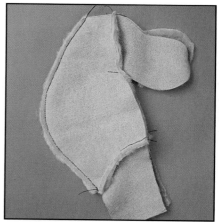

15 Stitch the back body pieces together along the seam line. Brush the seam.

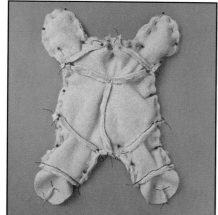

16 With right sides facing, pin the front body to the back body all the way round from neck to bottom of leg at **M**, from **M** to **M**, and from **M** around arm to neck.

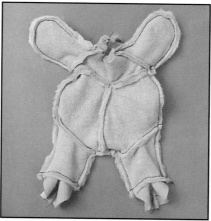

17 Stitch the front body to the back body along the seam line, leaving openings at the neck and leg ends.

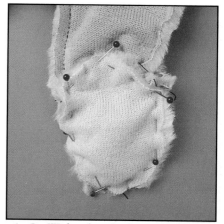

18 With right sides facing, pin the foot pads to the leg ends.

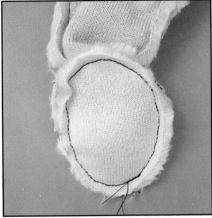

19 Stitch the foot pads to the leg ends, making the circles as even as possible.

20 Carefully snip the seams at the ease points.

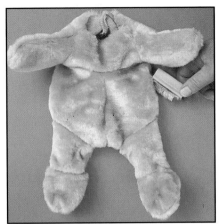

21 Turn the bear right side out and brush the seams.

22 With right sides facing, pin the back head pieces together from **C** to **D**.

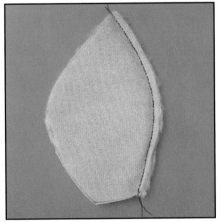

23 Stitch the back head pieces together along the seam line and brush the seam.

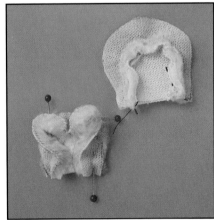

24 With right sides facing, pin and stitch the inner ears to the front ears from **W** to **W** and brush the seams.

25 With right sides facing, pin and stitch the front ears to the back ears.

26 Turn the ears right side out and brush the seams.

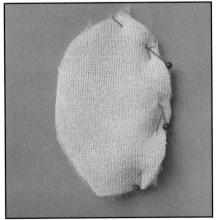

27 With right sides facing, pin the nose pieces together from **A** to **Y**.

28 Stitch the nose pieces together along the seam line and brush the seam.

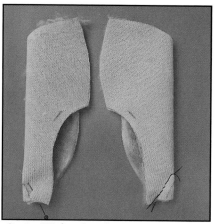

29 With right sides facing, pin and stitch the dart on the face from **Z** to **Z**.

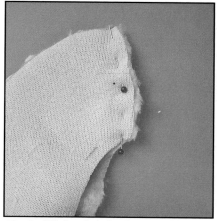

30 With right sides facing, fold the face in half and pin from **A** to **C**.

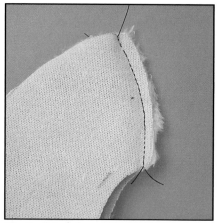

31 Stitch from **A** to **C** along the seam line and brush the seam.

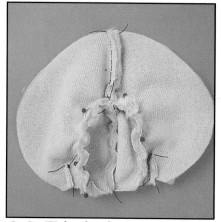

32 With right sides facing, pin the nose to the face from **A** to **B** and **B** to **A**.

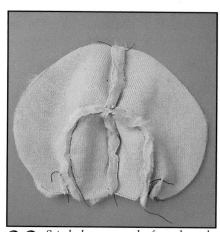

33 Stitch the nose to the face along the seam line and brush the seam.

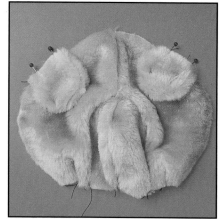

34 With the inner ears facing the right side of the face, pin the ears in the positions marked on the template.

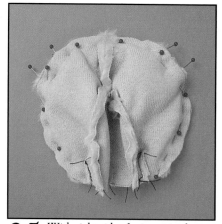

35 With right sides facing, pin the back head to the face from **C** to **E** and **E** to **C**.

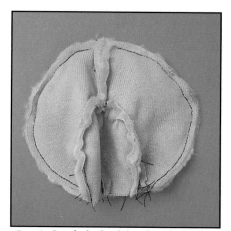

36 Stitch the back head to the face along the seam line. Turn right side out and brush the seam.

37 Insert the eyes and nose and embroider the mouth (see page 11).

38 Stuff the body and head with the filling until they are firm, but not too hard.

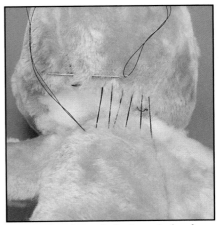

39 Hand sew the body to the head with ladder stitch (see page 8). Complete the bear by tying a bow of ribbon around its neck.

INDEX